A WHOLE SCHOOL APPROACH
TO PASTORAL CARE

Kogan Page Books for Teachers series
Series Editor: Tom Marjoram

A WHOLE SCHOOL APPROACH TO PASTORAL CARE

John McGuiness

Books for Teachers
Series Editor: Tom Marjoram

KOGAN PAGE

Para Amparo Gonzalez

First published in Great Britain in 1989 by
Kogan Page Limited, 120 Pentonville Road,
London N1 9JN

British Library Cataloguing in Publication Data
McGuinness, J.B. (John B.)
  A whole school approach to pastoral care.
  (Kogan Page books for teachers)
  1. Great Britain. Schools. Welfare work
  I. Title
  371.4'6

  ISBN 1–85091–589–X

Typeset by DP Photosetting, Aylesbury, Bucks
Printed and bound in Great Britain by
Biddles Ltd, Guildford

Contents

Acknowledgements

It has been a privilege on many INSET courses to share the perceptions of scores of teachers and colleagues who actually *do* what I write about. I offer this book as a stimulator of ideas, certainly not as a model. As both a parent of children in these teachers' care and as a member of the profession, I want teachers to remain problem-solvers not model-operators.

I would also like to thank my department's research committee for financial help in preparing the manuscript and our technical department, especially Judith Warner, for their artwork.

Finally, I would like to record my unqualified admiration for Susan Metcalf's ability to convert my illegible scrawl into typescript and my thanks to her for all her hard work on my behalf.

John McGuiness

Preface

This is a book about pastoral care; about what HMI called 'the central purpose of education' (DES, 1979). It is strange, a decade later, to remind ourselves of a time when such an emphasis could be given to the personal development of children. More recently, testing, vocationalism and central control have given instrumentality centre stage – people as tools and objects. Yet in a sense, the Inspectorate put their finger on a certain timeless element in educational practice, an element that transcends decades, governments, and social and economic change – the desire for our children to develop a sense of their own worth and a respect for the worth of other people. There will be few who would not see such an aim as central to our educational practice.

In what sense, then, can we regard 'the personal development of pupils' as the central purpose of education? Can our pastoral response really be accorded such importance? Ought we not to surrender that central ground to the task-masters, the functional architects of the so-called reform of education? Perhaps we can begin to look at the philosophical issue by asking this question: Do we want a society in which we value people on the basis of what they *are* or on the basis of what they can *do*? The question does not devalue either 'being' or 'doing' but it does challenge us to come clean on that area of our values. I recently attended a meeting to identify performance indicators for effective teaching. What evidence would we require to conclude that effective teaching had taken place? (This at university level.) One eminent colleague replied that he thought it was easy to establish such indicators – 'We take an average of the salaries of the students three years after they've left university.' To the objection that some of them might do VSO or become missionaries, he replied – 'You don't get Brownie points for helping old ladies across the road these days.' This was a national meeting of senior university staff – reduced to averaging salaries and Brownie points.

Yet that is only one area of the discussion on the centrality of young people's personal development. Beyond the philosophical issues underlying our perception of human beings as having either intrinsic or merely consequential value, is the clear psychological evidence that human beings perform tasks more effectively where certain emotional and social pre-conditions are met. Young people (and their teachers and Ministers) will perform tasks more competently when they perceive themselves as possessed of inviolable dignity and have developed a range of complex social and interpersonal skills. In that foundational sense, the personal development of our pupils must be given priority over task pursuit. For that reason, schools will pursue their proper and worthy academic objectives most effectively when the climate within which that task is pursued is infused with necessary emotional and social characteristics.

Few teachers can be complacent that some perfect state has been reached. Many resent the oversimplified dichotomies frequently used in the debate – testing or not testing, streaming or not, world of work or development of self, content or process, breadth or rigour. They may feed a media need for drama, a ministerial wish for headlines, but they are light-years away from the patient distillate which marks the reality of teaching practice. For the sake of pupils as much as for their teachers it is important to establish the facts about our comprehensive schools. *Our comprehensive schools are a success story.* Certainly not perfect, but currently giving more children, more success in more areas of endeavour than at any time in our educational history. Take a look at figures on their academic success. The Department of Education and Science produces, annually, national figures on activity in the education sector. (*Statistics in Education*, HMSO) Perusal of these government statistics indicate from 1970 to the present, clear evidence of dramatic academic achievements. At its most basic, we can see vast increases in academic success and reductions in numbers of young people without examination success. Simon's (1988) analysis of those figures shows that there was both a qualitative (over 5 O' levels, with grades A–C, increase by 45 per cent from 1970–84) and a quantitative (young people gaining one or more O' levels at D or E grade increase by 200 per cent) improvement. In addition, the number of young people leaving school without qualifications was about halved. If only other sectors of the country could show improvement levels of 50–200 per cent. Of course, teachers will rightly point out that there is far more to education than academic success, important though that is. It is the task of this book to examine that 'far more' – not in a dichotomous way, but in a way that builds on the solid achievements of the past 20 years, and tries to infuse the 1988 Education Act with a broader view of pupils' learning potential and a less content-centred view of the teacher's task.

As a defence of the 1988 Education Bill against the weight of the 18,000 replies to its initial presentation, the Secretary of State for Education on one occasion cited the Technical and Vocational Education Initiative as an example of an initiative opposed by the profession, but later accepted and indeed praised. As a parent of three children in the schools of the State Sector, I am grateful that the profession *did* soundly criticise the crude vocationalism of the early TVEI. The Secretary of State's pride in the scheme is now justified – an ill-thought out, hastily imposed and raw idea was 'subverted' by the profession; it was successfully 'educationalised'. Grubb and Lazerson (1981) in the USA provided some useful comment on the creeping vocationalisation of our secondary schools. They describe a situation very similar to Britain in the eighties, as they outline early American attempts to 're-establish the legitimacy of schooling'. Their paper suggests that to do this, businessmen had to be persuaded that school was able 'to increase the supply of skilled workers and to instil appropriate attitudes towards work, including anti-union sentiments' (p 92). The findings of the American experience is sobering in view of the TVEI's early emphasis on vocational training. Their comment that 'by promising solutions through the schools, more fundamental reforms – particularly in basic economic and political institutions – can be effectively postponed' may seem to take us away from schools. It does, however, remind us that scapegoating is always a diversionary tactic. More pertinent for our purposes, as teachers responsible for the *personal* development of our pupils, is a further challenge to the Act's conventional wisdom. 'By promoting an overly narrow concept of education and by creating a dual school system, vocational education was guilty of training students in ways that were too specific ... there was substantial evidence that trade and industrial training had no economic pay-off' (p 73). What our children need is an education which goes far beyond the fossil fuel of *content* to the renewable energy source of *process*; an education which values the personal as well as the academic, work on skills and attitudes as well as on knowledge and concepts.

This, then, is one educationalist's view of some of the context in which he tries to review developments in pastoral care. I spend some time on the contextual element because, just as our pupils' most significant learning of their worth is context-based, flowing through school ethos, learning climates and everyday interactions in school, so teachers' professional development is profoundly affected by the context within which they work. Pastoral care should encompass the whole of the educational community – there should be no opting out.

John McGuiness
Dec 1988

Chapter 1

No Opting Out

In introducing the concept of 'pastoral care' to a group of first-year student teachers, I asked them to describe their experience of it and to analyse its role in school. One student, with some wit and enviable precision, presented us with this summary of the discussion (Figure 1.1).

> Education is like a big sieve that we are all thrown into at the age of five. The teachers keep shaking the sieve, so that quite a few of us fall through the holes. Those who do fall are the failures and those who stick are the educational successes. Pastoral care acts as a kind of safety net under the sieve, as far as possible preventing serious damage to those who fall through, and even pushing one or two back through the holes into the sieve.

Pursuing the discussion a little further, I asked what proportion of pupils we might expect to fall through the holes. After all, a safety net is designed to prevent injury in the *unusual* situation of a fall. Were not the resources we deployed in school guidance services excessive if they were intended to catch only the occasional casualty?

The initial reaction to that suggestion varied, but the group quickly arrived at the consensus that the net was not catching the odd casualty, but rather a constant stream of casualties – perhaps as many as half our children were seen as casualties of the education system. These children were as Newsom had reminded us 'half our future'. The students then seemed content to leave the discussion there – the complex pastoral systems we offered were an appropriate response to the number of casualties they had identified. We had worked ourselves into the barely defensible position of having more artistes in the safety net than on the trapeze.

The student whose model began the discussion had described what might be called a 'remedial' view of pastoral care. In 1936, Bradshaw

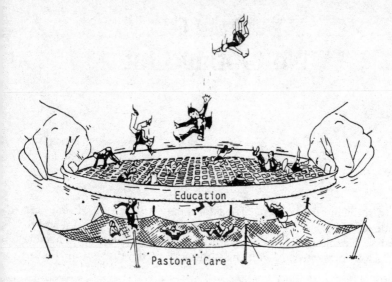

Figure 1.1. *Safety net view of pastoral care*

identified the function of pastoral care as delivering the pupil to the classroom 'in the optimum condition for instruction'. The fact that in 1977 R E Best could suggest that the teaching profession might regard pastoral care as 'a consciously evolved device for managing a potentially explosive situation' is an indication that the warm rhetoric about 'maximising individual potential' remained as empty then as it was in the 1930s. In fact, pastoral care still tends to be regarded and operated as a peripheral adjunct of the process of academic teaching: 'the element with which a breaking and unresponsive educational system grinds up students, without causing enough noise and commotion to arouse the sensitivities of those whose ideals and aspirations are being devoured along with the hopes of the student' (Blocher *et al.*, 1971). Such views of pastoral care regard 'instruction' as separable and separate from the general development of the child, and therein lies their crucial flaw.

Increasingly during the 1980s, the teaching profession began to develop a much more proactive view of that personal development of the child. We began to understand something of the concept of 'up-streaming'. Instead of constantly reacting to crisis, damage or deficiency in pupils (constructing a safety net with stronger rope, tighter weave and brighter paint) we began to pay attention to the trapeze. If so many people plunge regularly into the safety net, perhaps we ought to scrutinise the equipment. So began a detailed and professional analysis of the educational experiences of our pupils. Did it *have* to damage? What is it about children's experience of school that makes that experience so damaging to large numbers of them? We saw ourselves, gradually, in less dichotomous terms. Was I, as a modern linguist, somehow damaging half my pupils and then dashing off for my pastoral hat to mend the damage? Instead of plunging regularly into the stream to rescue drowning people, many teachers began to look upstream to see who or what was throwing them in. Not to engage in this exercise would be to opt for the safety net model of pastoral care – a wasteful model in that it is simply a rescue service. Resources are, of course, better deployed on prevention than cure. There is a real sense in which it could be argued that the dichotomous approach to pastoral care, running it as a parallel and subordinate adjunct to the academic work of the school, leads us to 'plan' the failure of large numbers of pupils (McGuiness and Craggs, 1986; Schostak, 1983; Hemmings, 1980), safe in the knowledge that our pastoral rescue service will pick up the pieces. We could feel absolved from the responsibility of carefully scrutinising the (unintended) damage to some children which results from our academic endeavours.

The Inspectorate's survey of secondary education (1979) observed that 'in general, schools placed much greater emphasis on fostering the personal development of their pupils through pastoral care than through their curriculum' and recommended that three-quarters of the schools surveyed should give more detailed attention to the ways in which the curriculum could serve pupil needs in the area of *personal* development. Although the phrase is not used, they are recommending a guidance-oriented curriculum and unequivocally rejecting the dichotomous approach to pastoral care described by my student, Bradshaw in the 1930s, and still used by a large number of schools in the 1980s. That task, clearly identified by the Inspectorate in several curriculum documents since 1979, has been zealously pursued by the profession, despite a counter-productive push from the politicians at the DES towards a narrow, more instrumental view of the curriculum. Thus we have a pupil-centred movement in initiatives like GCSE, TVEI and Profiling meeting the subject-centred, market-place movement of the new Education Act. What place will there be for the less able, those with special needs, those with limited resources in the broadest sense, in this new dispensation? What limiting of perspectives, lowering of horizons and wastage of talent will occur if the profession fails to take this Act by the scruff of its neck to breath some educational life into it? There is a real danger that we will push ourselves back into a situation roundly criticised by Newsom (1963) as 'wastage humanly and economically speaking'. We must examine critically the consequences of placing vast numbers of the young people in our schools in the impossible situation of being judged by criteria which bear little relationship to their talents and potential. Teachers know and are responding to the reality that such children, who are invited day after day for 15,000 hours to contemplate their worthlessness in terms of what the new dispensation in education evidently prizes most highly, will be shamefully betrayed. Many initiatives undertaken by the profession to respond to these children's educational needs are jeopardised by the narrowness and inflexibility of the new provisions. As a profession, we had begun to come to terms with the magnitude of the task given us by society, which asks us to undertake 'secondary eduction for all' to the age of 16. We were not asked to pursue only academically high standards – even if we toss in the pursuit of vocationally appropriate skills for the less able; we are asked to 'educate' our pupils. I will resist the temptation to attempt definitions of the word, partly because there is such disagreement that the debate would be fruitless, but mainly because a recent government report gives a generally acceptable official version. The Warnock Report on special education chose to regard as being in special educational need those children whose ability to 'learn to be adults' was impaired. It seems that society has given its teachers the task of helping children 'learn to be adults'. We have come a long way since 1979. Recognition of the complexity of that task has led us to enrich and expand the offerings we make to all our pupils, not at the expense of academic results, which as the Preface indicates have improved dramatically, but by refining our awareness of the potential of the academic curriculum for delivering pastoral care.

Hargreaves (1967) and Lacey (1970) had exposed the old grammar school selective system for what it was – an indefensible wastage of natural talent. Not only did it reject at age 11 about 80 per cent of the population, it also managed to persuade the lower attainees of our most able 20 per cent that they too were failures. Teachers accepted the broader, more demanding teaching responsibilities by creating strategies designed to pursue the new objectives. It was like trying to row a boat stuck in a sand-bar. Much earlier, in 1949, Dent had written: 'Everyone agrees, at least in theory, that secondary education for all does not mean merely modifying or watering down the grammer school curriculum ... But what hardly anyone seems to be prepared to face is the hard fact that to provide suitable education for all children is so utterly different a problem from providing a special kind of education for a few selected children as to constitute an entirely new problem.'

Thirty years after Dent we were beginning to face what he describes as an 'utterly different problem' by performing what he had described as 'the almost superhuman feat of thinking outside the categories of thought in which practically all of our educational thinking has been done'. New areas of study, new approaches to pedagogy, much greater emphasis on pupil-teacher relationships were springing up all over the country. Of course, some teachers rejected the new tasks – 'I teach physics, I'm no half-baked social worker' – unaware that beyond the professional dereliction involved in such statements lay the psychological impossibility of divorcing academic activity from social and emotional consequences. Such teachers are increasingly rare, but may increase in numbers as the Secretary of State plants his system firmly back on the sand-bar. There is a sense in which the Act will encourage that small number of teachers who lacked commitment to the educational changes of the last 30 years, despite continuing to write off up to half of their pupils as an alternative to criticising themselves or the 'watered-down grammar school curriculum'.

Change

There is a story current in educational circles of the headteacher who, at his retirement dinner, declared proudly, 'I have never changed my teaching since I qualified – and I have found myself in the fashion twice in 40 years.' It could be a proud boast of refusal to bow to the fickle winds of fashion from a person who lived in a stable, predictable and acceptable world, but one must ask how such a posture could be defended in a dynamic, unpredictable and impermanent world. Change is a consistent phenomenon of our world and we, as we help our pupils become adults, need to respond to that change.

John Elliot-Kemp, a management consultant, once described teaching as the kind of change in which the learner is invited to move from security to insecurity, from comfort to discomfort, from a degree of competence to a position of relative incompetence. Thus an organisation, a professional, a pupil will be invited to set on one side the initial competence and security of the already learned and to undertake a journey through incompetence and discomfort towards new learning. We've all done that; leaving the comfort of English to taste the discomfort of our incompetence in French, or whatever; leaving the

17

sand-bar of solid grammar school realities to toss incompetently on the high sea of new comprehensive schools, or quitting the predictability of GCE and clear syllabuses for the more unpredictable, pupil-centred GCSE and TVEI.

The key issue with regard to the facilitation of change for the teacher, the manager or the learner is to create a situation in which those who are to change undertake that journey with confidence, even eagerness. Thus our daily invitation to our pupils to involve themselves in change (ie learn) leaves them asking the question: 'Why should I stir my bones out of this comfortable "known" to set off towards an uncomfortable "unknown"?' It is a familiar enough question – we have posed it regularly ourselves as we have faced the constant changes in our profession over the last three decades. The social psychologists suggest that people pursue change constructively when they feel that they are in safe, risk-free environments. They resist change, opt out or even sabotage it when they are under threat, feel exposed or under-supported. While this applies to commercial and industrial organisations as well as schools, to adults as well as children, I would like to examine its application with reference to our pupils. In our pursuit of academic tasks, we daily invite our pupils to engage in the kind of risk-taking we call learning. They will do it more happily and more effectively when their teachers can make the environment within which the task is pursued a safe place.

It is very rare to find a teacher who is task-incompetent, ie a chemist who knows no chemistry, a linguist who cannot speak foreign languages, a mathematician who cannot add up. I recall a geography student of ours, who failed his probationary year, writing: 'I did a three-year honours degree in geography, a year learning about the textbooks, the syllabuses, the approaches to geography, but in the classroom the kids didn't want to know.' He certainly was a competent geographer but he could not teach – he was unsuccessful in inviting his pupils to engage in that special kind of risk-taking we call learning. In the terms of the social psychologists he was an effective task leader (I know this field, where to go, how to approach it – follow me) but an ineffective social leader (in pursuing this task with me, you will be safe, not humiliated, not at risk, enhanced not diminished as a human being). The effective teacher combines task competence and social competence. To be skilled in one of these kinds of leadership and not the other vastly diminishes teacher effectiveness. The excellent physicist who cannot relate to pupils in a way that creates a safe environment for them will lose all those children for whom physics is a daunting opportunity to appear foolish (the majority). Equally the highly

Thesis

supportive, socially skilled teacher who is not an expert in his subject will lack the ability to use effectively the motivational drive which comes from good teacher–pupil relationships. The pastoral infusion of the whole curriculum is not a frill or option; it is the oxygen essential for the learning process to occur.

There is such a wealth of research consistently pushing us towards the idea that certain kinds of relationships are essential for effective task performance in groups that it is astonishing that we still need to make the case. The work of Abercrombie (1979) presents cogent evidence that sensitively led groups change learner response from one of mere acceptance to one of understanding and mastery of new material. Heath (1977), Kohlberg (1977) and Nicholson (1970) had earlier, after careful research, come to the conclusion that academic achievement made no *independent* contribution to success in life. None of these researchers could find any predictive value in a pupil's academic performance on later 'life success'. It was not that clever children did not make it in life – their findings indicate forcefully that clever children were successful *only when they also possessed certain socio-emotional characteristics*, and that those children who were not clever by conventional criteria were successful in life when they possessed these social and emotional qualities. The consistent correlation in each study was between those children who demonstrate social skills, confidence and a sense of personal dignity, and later successful adult life. It seems that the most precious gift we can give to children at school is not simply or even primarily academic success, but social and emotional maturity. The centrality of the social leadership skills of the teacher is indisputable.

My work as a counselling psychologist takes me into analysing the way in which human beings can help each other grow (ie learn, change). I have recently worked with business and commercial managers, GPs, nurses, careers officers as well as teachers. There is an increasing awareness in all these groups that improved relationship skills will enhance task performance. Poor relationship skills will diminish it. Thus an exercise which I regularly do with the groups I meet is as follows:

Please decide with your neighbour who will be A, who B. If it helps you concentrate, close your eyes, and bring to mind any teacher from years past who has in some way damaged, diminished, humiliated or hurt you. Relive some of your encounters, run that person through the fingers of your mind.

Now A should invest B with the personality of that remembered destructive teacher. Personalise your response. Don't say 'Mr Smith hurt

Thesis 1

me when he used to ...'; say 'You damaged me when ... because ...' You have two minutes to vent your anger.

The noise is enormous. There is an explosion of anger which has been suppressed for years. It is a half-jocular, frequently deeply serious articulation of long-buried resentments. The participants are teachers, doctors, businessmen – probably from that able, privileged 20 per cent who were supposed to benefit from selective education. What would the other 80 per cent have to tell us?

> Right. Close your eyes again. This time think of any teacher about whom you could say, he or she was special to me, helped me to grow, to realise my talent, to see wider possibilities. Relive some of your encounters with that person. Now repeat the same process as before, telling your partner, 'You were special for me when/because ...'

Sad to say, this is quieter, less vociferous and occasionally a participant will say, 'I can't think of anyone like that.'

What the groups are doing is to bring to mind some foundational characteristics of teachers at either pole of a continuum. They are pushed in a brief fantasy to crystallise some key teaching characteristics. The final part of the exercise is to draw from the group examples of those characteristics. Browsing through my files I have selected the following list as typical.

Destructive teachers ...	*... while good teachers*
bully	are sympathetic
lash you verbally	listen
are violent	make you feel good about yourself
humiliate	inspire
are wrapped up in themselves	care
have favourites	are humorous, not cruel
are impatient	respect your ideas
make you feel guilty	have time for you
flaunt authority	encourage
make you feel useless	are interested in *you*

There is a remarkable similarity in the lists generated by different groups, even across professions. Thus the issue of good/bad manager, good/bad ward sister, good/bad doctor and good/bad teacher shows clearly that in the final analysis we identify social and emotional characteristics, not task characteristics. Of course, we value task competence (passing exams, nursing effectively, diagnostic ability, producing goods) but all groups, in my experience, identify as a central and generic hope that the task pursuit should occur in a respecting and respectful interpersonal encounter. The quality of the relationship *radically* affects the success of task pursuit. It is reassuring that the *experience* of professionals matches so closely the findings of the research.

It becomes increasingly difficult, then, for any teacher to opt out of the personal development of pupils. The delivery potential (positive or negative) of the academic subjects in the pastoral area is difficult to deny. To maintain the stance, 'I'm a linguist – I'm not concerned with the kids' social and emotional development' is the professional equivalent of a doctor who prescribes medicine with no regard for side effects. 'Take these pills for your heart – they'll rot your liver, but I'm a heart man myself. I believe Jones is good on livers.' Ridiculous? 'Sit in my French class. You're pretty useless at it and will undoubtedly feel inadequate, but we have this great pastoral system that will buck you up. I'm a linguist myself. Don't know much about this pastoral business. I believe Mr Smith is good on the pastoral bits.'

	Knowledge	Skills	Attitudes
Academic	eg Facts 　　Concepts 　　Understanding 　　Information 1	eg Using facts 　　Logical skills 　　Study skills 　　Search skills 2	eg Curiosity 　　Enthusiasm 　　Love of a subject 　　Risk-taking 3
Social	eg The structure of 　　our society 　　Role of women 4	eg Ability to be a 　　team member 　　Ability to lead 　　Ability to follow 　　Ability to 　　establish/ 　　maintain 　　relationships 5	eg Attitudes to 　　gender, race 　　Attitudes to 　　industry and 　　academe 6
Emotional	eg The answer to 　　the question 　　'Who am I?' 　　My strengths, 　　weaknesses 7	eg To be assertive, 　　accepting of 　　self 　　To be able to 　　delay 　　gratification 8	eg To accept, 　　respect self 　　To accept, 　　respect others 9

Figure 1.2. *Consequences of teaching: the complex dynamic of the classroom*

What we have done is identify the complexity of the teaching/ classroom dynamic. In the past we have been able to pretend that all that happened in a classroom was academic learning. We are increasingly aware that there is more to it than that (Figure 1.2). The consistent, cumulative input of material beyond the academic makes it a professional responsibility that teachers scrutinise the *full* range of outcomes of the teaching activity. We must not become so locked into our academic activity that we fail to see the full extent of the consequences that activity has on our pupils.

As teachers, most of us are trained to respond to cells 1 and 2, paying a little attention to 3. We are beginning to realise that 1, 2, and 3 can be totally undermined if 4 to 9 are not carefully planned. How many girls have their talent crushed by the unthinking sexism of their teachers? How many pupils learn early the lesson that caution, keeping one's head below the parapet, will ensure a quiet life? These are issues to which we must return throughout this book. They relate to the vast increase in responsibility which has been given to the profession in recent years – not simply GCE/GCSE, not only the introduction of TVEI, far beyond the requirement of regular testing. We must also work on issues of race, gender, child sexual abuse, employability – the list is endless. The impositions occur, too, at a time of falling resources, lowered status and the assailed morale described in the Preface. To use the framework of the last few pages, we are asked to pursue new tasks in a totally inappropriate social climate. The temptation to resist, opt out or sabotage must be high.

The defensive reaction of teachers to this pressure has led them to point outside the school to explain the problems they face within it. If the causes of the problems identified so acutely by the media lie outside the school, teachers can breathe a little easier, feel less threatened and answer the critics. Thus children who present difficulties in the classroom have been designated maladjusted, subnormal or unbalanced. They have been described as the product of poor living conditions, negative family attitudes or the poverty trap, and so consigned to the psychologists and sociologists, no longer the responsibility of the school.

In the dichotomous, political, educational world in which we live, the question is also being asked whether we are simply picking up the less attractive aspects of the 'Thatcher generation'. Acquisitiveness, competition, strength, achievement, individualism can too easily slide into greed, bullying, contempt for others, a win-at-all-costs, selfish approach to life. Teachers do see themselves cast unjustly in the role of scapegoat for a society which has lost its confidence in former values.

It is important that in the battle to maintain carefully constructed educational gains neither the profession nor the Government averts its gaze from the casualties among our pupils.

There can be no doubt that we do face in the classroom pupils who are psychologically inept or whose environment militates against their school success, and for such pupils the out-of-school responses of Child Guidance Units, Educational Priority Areas and the whole range of psycho-social referral possibilities are totally appropriate. I would argue, however, that such children cause a small proportion of our problems, that most of our in-school problems come from children for whom referral is not only not possible, but also not appropriate. Davie *et al.* (1972) are quoted in Jones (1975) and report that referral to a Child Guidance Unit, even for disturbed children, is the exception rather than the rule because of the enormous case loads carried by the school psychologists, and thus, whether we like it or not, most of our problem children remain the responsibility of the ordinary school.

Secondary education for all up to the age of 16, particularly in its 'comprehensive' form, requires that teachers tackle the educational needs of the full range of children. It is not that 'subject specialists' are a thing of the past, it is simply that they are now asked by the society that employs them to be more than expert in a subject. They are charged with helping children in their personal as well as their academic growth. The Inspectorate's working paper *Curriculum 11–16* (1977) emphasised the crucial nature of full staff involvement in pastoral care, arguing that social objectives 'must be realised through the nature of the personal relationships in the classroom ... and through the daily example of all the adults with whom the pupils are in contact'.

It is the acceptance of this role, and the structuring of a child's school experience to accommodate it, that is the first vital step in a preventive approach to pastoral care. I say 'preventive' rather than 'remedial' because I hope to show that many of the problems which occur in school, and which eventually require 'remedial' responses from the school, can be pre-empted. Hargreaves (1976a, b and c) set the cat among the pigeons by suggesting that external psychological and sociological explanations of pupil failure offer at best only part of the answer. He suggests that the defensive ploy, of pointing outside our schools to explain failure inside, has blinkered us to the possibility that the school itself may produce pathogenic effects on the pupils. Thus we arrive at the first major question a school staff needs to examine. It is a question which demands that degree of security which is a hallmark of the professionalism which permits effective self-criticism.

'To what extent does this school *cause* the problems it purports to solve?' To tackle this question effectively will involve the school in a detailed analysis of:

1. The nature of its pupils.
2. The intentional *and* accidental effects of its curriculum.
3. The skills and attitudes of its teaching staff.

Only in this way can the interaction in the school be evaluated against clearly stated outcomes in pupil behaviour.

Who are our pupils?

Detailed investigations by Tibble (1964) show clearly that it is not simply the maladaptive child who needs or wants help from and involvement with adults. Extensive conversations with teenagers led him to conclude: 'All of the adolescent groups provided evidence of this need to be regarded as persons, as individuals, as different from each other, to be taken seriously, have reasons given ... There was evidence from all the young people that they felt the need for more guidance and preparation for what lay ahead.' Such, then, are the objects of our professional activity.

Adolescence is a time of change and doubt and, although recent research indicates a major divergence of opinion about the degree of cultural discontinuity between adolescence and adulthood, the generation gap (Erikson, Piaget, Coleman and Sherif appear to emphasise the gap between adolescent and adult, while Musgrave, Jahoda and Warren see it as exaggerated), most seem to agree that it is a developmental process which sees the transformation of the child into the adult. Brammer and Shostrum (1968, 1982) reconcile the two opinions when they refer to growth as an 'integrative and disintegrative process'. They comment that before adult patterns can become operative, childhood patterns must be disrupted. Our pupils are involved in this key task during their secondary school years, and the school is in a position either to help or hinder the process. It is a process regularly observed by parents and teachers – the young child delights both of them by his display of increasing mastery over his world from birth to 11 years old. Obvious strides in physical prowess, verbal skill and cognitive ability take place. Less obvious, but no less real, developments in emotional control and social confidence lead the child to a growing sense of control over his world and comfort in it. But it is a mastery and a comfort that has to be shattered and reconstructed in adolescence.

That brilliant footballer from the junior school, who leaves his primary school in July, goes to his new secondary school in September with legs several centimetres longer, and his brain still working with the old expectations. Physical control is diminished and doubts ensue, and those fine skills have to be learned all over again. Body awareness and self-consciousness loom large; a growing ability to abstract and hypothesise certainly expands horizons, but makes him feel less significant, less in control and less sure. New emotions and social worries emerge (acne, pubic hair, menstruation, needing or not needing a bra – all frequently the subject of surface humour) and can be the source of deep, painful anxieties.

Children cope with these difficulties with a wide variety of strategies – withdrawal into a protective, timid, almost submissive courtesy, or with a brash, surface cockiness, perhaps with a highly structured inflexible external control, or even with a complete lapse into uncontrolled behaviour reminiscent of early childhood. Whatever the steps the youngster takes to cope with his new situation, the school needs to keep a careful watching brief to allow the fullest possible reliance on personal resources, but be able to offer strong support as soon as it becomes necessary.

As teachers it is so easy to become insensitive, simply by over-exposure, to the sudden self-doubt which so frequently accompanies adolescence. When we combine that self-doubt with the confused values presented to the young by our society, and add the pressure of passing from a relatively small unit in primary school to a huge, perhaps less personal, unit in the comprehensive school, we begin to understand some of the difficulties facing the youngsters in our classes. It cannot be without significance that several studies show that, while suicide rates nationally have declined, for young people between 15 and 20 they have increased 55 per cent (Clegg and Megson, 1973). Subsequent figures from the Samaritans suggest that adolescents remain an inordinately suicide-prone group in our society.

If the school, then, is to undertake successfully the task of helping its pupils 'learn to be adults', it must broaden its view of the child beyond the narrow confines of academic potential to include the full range of their developmental potential. Teachers must understand and respond to the mechanisms which permit or prevent each pupil's growth as a person.

In a real sense Musgrave (1967) was correct in his assertion that 'adolescence' is an artificial construct, yet the concept does represent a reality in highly industrialised nations. 'Learning to be an adult' in Samoa or New Guinea does not involve learning the vast range of complex coping skills needed by adults in our society. The circumcision and two weeks' 'rites of passage' is indeed adequate preparation for full participation in adult life in a primitive society, but our society has found it a necessary part of socialisation to offer to (indeed require from) its young an extended transitional period before we are willing to admit them to adulthood. This extension is deemed necessary to allow for survival in a technological society. It involves much more than academic preparation, and much of it must take place in school.

The very complexity of our society permits the young person a wide range of possible roles. Anna Freud (1968) refers to the changeableness of young people as 'commonplace'. She describes the mercurial, contrasting, often contradictory behaviour that adolescents show to adults – 'excessively egotistic, regarding themselves as the centre of the universe' and 'capable of ... much self-sacrifice and devotion' or 'submission to some self-chosen leader' and 'defiant rebellion against any and every authority'. She describes their 'light-hearted optimism and indefatigable enthusiasm' which is followed and preceded by 'blackest pessimism and apathy'. It is a picture that will strike a responsive chord for many who work with young people.

A description of adolescent behaviour is easy – an explanation of it less so. However, if we are to make a curriculum response to the teenage pupil which matches or parallels his development, we must go to the theorists to seek insight into what is happening. There is no 'right answer' or complete explanation, but the following views shed some light on why adolescents are as they are.

One possible explanation for the phenomena described by Freud, and experienced, one suspects, by all secondary school-teachers, is found in the work of Erik Erikson (1965). He suggests that personality development, the route to adulthood, occurs as a result of the way the individual negotiates a series of 'identity crises' which take place at key points in his life. Thus in infancy a child establishes 'basic trust' or 'basic mistrust' *vis-à-vis* the world. The determining factor in this first identity crisis is the extent to which the child's world is comforting or threatening. So the level of consistency and security in the infant's feeding, sleeping and handling will crucially affect his view of the world. Kellmer-Pringle (1965) points to the almost frightening control parents have of infants – they govern almost totally the child's access to and experience of pleasure and pain. How often is the adolescent, who is defiant and antagonistic towards authority in general, playing out a lesson learned in that first identity crisis when it is found that the world is not a place to be trusted?

Toilet training, speech development, mobility, beginning school – all critical events in Erikson's analysis – elicit responses from the child which affect his adjustment to his world. Eventually, as cognitive skills develop, the child arrives at the adolescent crisis. The problem life tosses to the child at this juncture is that he should begin to look for an answer to the question 'Who am I?'. Erikson sees the individual here moving between 'role confusion' (trying out many parts – the mercurial aspect of adolescence) and having a clear, consistent comprehension of who he is. This point – ego identity – is the point at which adulthood begins. Gone are the doubts of adolescence, the searching around for an appropriate, comfortable 'me', the need to do down others who seem so much more comfortable with themselves. It is the base on which friendships are made, marriage is sought, work is embarked upon and, in a sense, the culmination of 12 years of schooling.

The child, then, enters adolescence with an imprecisely defined sense of self, but eager to experiment with various observed roles, trying them on, as it were, in an attempt to reach that degree of precision in self-awareness which constitutes the end of adolescence. Role experimentation is a necessary expansion and exploration by the child of his potential. It can explain much of that 'commonplace' fickleness described by Freud, and might draw teachers' attention to an awareness that a rejection of role-playing, a refusal to allow it, represents a thwarting of a normal developmental process. But more of that when we consider the curriculum.

When Erikson speaks of ego identity he means that the individual has achieved the ability to answer the question 'Who am I?'. Of growing significance as an extension of our understanding of adolescence is the work of a group of psychologists who have been called 'self-theorists'. Their contribution to our attempt to understand our secondary school pupils challenges our ingenuity as teachers enormously. They take us on, beyond the fundamental issue of helping pupils tackle the question 'Who am I?', to the problem of individual self-esteem. As the pupil begins to crystallise a sense of self, what is his response to it? Does he like what he sees, is it acceptable, or does he recoil from it? Answers to these questions are vital, since the basic postulate of the self-theorists is that the single most important task of a human being is to establish and maintain self-esteem. This is so vital to our psychological health that if our self-esteem comes under attack our defence reaction is virtually automatic. Quite simply it asserts that if someone is making us feel small, insignificant or unimportant we *need* to fight back. So an institution which patently gives value only to one type of success (academic) implicitly devalues and undermines those children who are unable to achieve in that area. Those children *need* to fight back – and do so with displays of aggression, disrupting and consequently devaluing the source of the attack. Truancy and even day-dreaming can on occasion be seen as withdrawals from the school's persistent statement to some pupils that they are without value.

Even in the realm of cognitive development we find that the refined, more sophisticated skills of the adolescent are possible sources of trouble. Piaget argues that the adolescent needs to reject adult constructions of reality and complete the establishment of his own independence. Just as the young child finds it difficult to see physically from another person's viewpoint, so the adolescent, freed from the concrete world by his ability to hypothesise, finds it difficult to accept any hypothesis but his own. Piaget and Inhelder (1958) reject the idea that this desire and ability to construct theories about the world is the prerogative of bright children: 'Look at the reactions of adolescent workers, apprentices or peasants – we can recognise the same phenomena.' With cognitively less developed children, he argues, the search for independence will appear in terms of actions rather than ideas. It is a long way from Piaget to punk rock, but the latter can surely be construed in Piagetian terms as an eloquent rejection of adult constructions of reality.

Broadly, then, we might expect the adolescent to display a measure of unpredictable, contradictory behaviour which would indicate a search for a stable sense of self. He would seek to establish a growing sense of autonomy, rejecting adult views in a narrow, pedantic way, and he would desperately need, in the midst of this struggle for an independent self, to maintain a high degree of self-esteem. The 'map' of adolescent development is shown as Figure 1.3 fills in some of the detail, revealing to us the enormous potential and complexity of our charge. The school's task is not to offer him a watered-down grammar school curriculum, but a purpose-built comprehensive curriculum which would encourage and promote all the developments outlined in the table, facilitating the search for an independent self and helping to maintain and enhance self-esteem.

When the Inspectorate (1979) described the personal and social development of pupils as 'the central purpose of education' (p 206) they were not suggesting that academic excellence should not be a goal for schools. But they did suggest, in passage after passage, that the pursuit of academic goals and of social goals as separable and separate, either at school level or in the individual classroom, was doomed to failure.

Curriculum – what do our pupils need from us?

Pastoral care in school stands or fails on the care with which the *curriculum* is constructed and monitored. Teachers need to subject to a meticulous analysis not only the content of courses taught in their school, but the teaching methods used, the structures and relationships within which teaching occurs, and the organisation and administration which facilitates teaching activity. DES investigations suggest that schools will point frequently to an extensive range of courses – natural sciences, humanities, modern languages, mathematical sciences – as evidence of a well-balanced curriculum, with only the most scanty consideration of the 'hidden curriculum' effects of teaching methods, pupil grouping and school ethos (*Aspects of Secondary Education in England*, Chapter 9, para 2.35).

Law (1979) unerringly puts his finger on the issue:

> Teachers teach not only what they intend to teach in the structure of their curriculum: they teach other things as well – about what is valued and what is not valued, about what kind of attention gets paid to what kind of student ... Not only the classrooms but the corridors, the sports fields, the assembly halls, the dining rooms, the trophy cupboards, the honour boards and the courtyards are filled with such informal messages containing meanings beyond the overtly declared and formally acknowledged functions they appear to be fulfilling.

No professional can allow effects to emerge from his activity without seeking to control those effects. Yet schools do, for example, continue to communicate, unintentionally but effectively, the sexual chauvinism which has given girls second-class status for so long. Schools frequently state in their handbooks their intention to produce 'mature, considerate young adults', yet they regularly offer little dignity and few opportunities for decision-making. Industry complains of yet another piece of meta-learning – that somehow pupils acquire the conviction that the factory is less desirable than academe as a vocational aspiration. To offer a fully professional service, the school must seek out these hidden effects and evaluate them with the same rigour as the rest of the curriculum.

These are questions, areas to be analysed by the teachers themselves. No outsider could offer useful suggestions about answers. A teacher-centred, information-based, note-taking approach, for example, in a classroom containing children whose writing skills and concentration are poor will not achieve even an academic objective – and it will probably produce negative social and emotional results. Equally, an

Child age	Comments	Erikson A	Super B	Piaget C	Blocher D	Havighurst E	Kohlberg F	Brammer and Shostrum G	Major 'coping skills' summary H
7	Although developmentally these stages are associated with 6–12-year-olds teachers will be aware that many 12–16-year-olds are deficient in these skills	Increasing ability to take initiatives – enthusiasm. A willingness to plan and attack tasks with resourcefulness and resilience. An ability to cope with failures	Growth stage – Self-concept develops by identification with key figures in family/school. (cf. Ginzburg – Fantasy work choices)	A move away from 'intuitive' transductive thought to logical, though concretely based, thinking	Learning to read, calculate, to value self, to delay gratification. Control emotions. To abstract and formulate values	Physical skills, wholesome self-concept, age-mate relationships. Sex-role. Academic skills (basic). Values developed – more independence – positive attitudes to groups (peer group important)	Awareness of and response to family, peer expectations, seeking approval of significant others. Awareness of 'social order' and response to it	Conformity stage 'Gang' influence, particularly among boys. Expanding potentiality can be stifled or fixed at this level	1. Self-esteem 2. Literacy 3. Numeracy 4. Concrete logical thinking 5. Initiative taking 6. Work 'fantasy' 7. Gratification delay 8. Response to 'social order'
10			Tentative vocational choice based on needs, interests. Value factor appears in tentative job choices	An increasing ability to think in the abstract, to speculate. A tendency to reconstruct the environment cognitively	Establish identity, learn sex-role, develop relationship and responsibility to work study, develop values. Use groups	Interaction with peers – acceptance of one's physique. Sex-role. Emotional independence of parents. Preparation for job/family life, civic competence	Beginning attempt to define moral principles apart from supporting authority – a 'contract' model of duty. Reciprocity	Transition stage Efforts to break away from family, establish sexual identity. Intense feelings of separateness and individuality	9. Formal logical thinking 10. Social skill with peers 11. Tentative vocational choice 12. Emerging moral principles 13. Sex identity 14. Move to independence

	A tendency to explore many roles as part of an attempt to answer the question 'who am I?'. An approximate arrival at ego identity	Transitional vocational selection – more weight to capacity, job availability, and *reality*. Some attempts to implement self-concept	A move away from the 'present' focused cognitive stage as the young person tends to 'think beyond the present' – but with an increasing sense of reality	Identity as a worker – use group less; emotional autonomy; to be productive in work situations	Developing a philosophy of life – acquiring a set of values and an ethical system of socially responsible behaviour	Development of conscience or principle orientation, awareness of logical consistency, universality as a norm for action, a 'trust' model of behaviour	*Synthesis stage* Begins to see life as a unit from birth to death. Profound questions on human relations, social reality, life, work, and sexuality need to be answered	
16 Some teachers would argue that many of the features of these stages demand sophisticated cognitive skills which many children never acquire. Group work offers a more concrete, less sophisticated situation for developing coping skills **19**	cf. Esp. Erikson, E H (1965) *Childhood and Society*, Penguin	cf. Esp. Super, D E (1957) *The Psychology of Careers*, Harper & Row	cf. Esp. Beard, R M (1969) *An Outline of Piaget's Developmental Psychology for Teachers*, Routledge & Kegan Paul	cf. Esp. Blocher, D (1974) *Development Counselling*, Ronald	cf. Esp. Havinghurst, R J (1953) *Human Development Education*, Longman, Green & Co	cf. Esp. Graham, D (1972) *Moral Learning and Development*, Batsford	cf. Esp. Brammer, L M and Shostrum, E L (1968) *Therapeutic Psychology*, 2nd edn, Prentice-Hall	15. Emotional autonomy 16. Ability to hypothesise 17. Move to ego identification 18. Increasing sense of reality – particularly reference to world of work 19. Moral autonomy

Figure 1.3. *Who are our pupils? An overview of potential areas of development*

entirely concrete, reality-focused lesson might well frustrate able children who are at home speculating, hypothesising and theorising. Neither approach is completely the answer – but *accidental* exposure to one or the other is not acceptable as an offering from a professional body – the planned use of methods is one sign of aware teaching.

In the Inspectorate's 1977 Working Paper, *Curriculum 11–16*, the following statement clearly identifies a curriculum baseline: 'A precondition of active, purposeful study is the development of a caring atmosphere and of correspondingly good personal relationships.'

If we accept this, we are accepting the importance, indeed the necessity, of the establishment of certain social conditions as a prerequisite of effective curriculum operation.

In a small survey containing questions on the planning of socio-emotional outcomes of the curriculum, McGuiness (1977) met with considerable resistance from schools to his questions on that aspect of the curriculum (as indeed did the DES in its own larger 1977 questionnaire), in what was perhaps another manifestation of the defensive reaction to outsiders probing school performance. What did emerge from the sample was the vagueness of the statements by schools on their socio-emotional objectives compared with the clarity of aims in the academic sphere. Structures and organisation in the schools distinguished clearly (and saw little point in integrating) the academic and socio-emotional development of children. Of course, there were notable exceptions to this pattern, but the general indication was that the 'watered-down grammar school curriculum' with its cognitive, academic emphasis still flourished in our comprehensive schools.

School favouritism towards academically able children identified by Hargreaves (1967) builds into school curricula a bias towards purely academic objectives, and it can be no part of my task to diminish the concern schools have for academic excellence. (Indeed, the contrary is so – I would like schools to ask whether they are fully extending the most able children they have.) It is important, however, in view of this academic bias, to draw attention to the likely consequences of placing an academically less able child (the 'half our future' of Newsom's Report) in the impossible situation of being judged by criteria which bear little relationship to his overall potential. It must be added that a disservice is also done to the academically able child if he is encouraged to think that excellence or worth as a person correlates with academic ability.

That a balanced curriculum should contain deliberately constructed strategies to develop academic *and* socio-emotional competence is indicated by studies like those of Hargreaves (1967) and Lawrence

(1973). Lawrence produced significant improvements in children's reading ability by exposing poor readers to esteem-enhancing activities, thus pointing clearly to the effect of socio-emotional development on a specific academic skill. Hargreaves observed the reverse relationship – the effect of inadequate academic skill on socio-emotional development: 'The boys in lower streams not only regard the teacher less favourably, but also perceive their relationships with teachers as much less adequate.'

The dilemma facing teachers can seem paralysing – pursuit of high academic standards will benefit the able pupil, yet at the same time force the less able child into a position where he cannot fail to see himself as worthless in *terms of what the school evidently prizes*. Should the school, then, opt for a mediocre standard in academic matters, so that no one need feel threatened, or accept the danger of producing thousands of alienated children for whom school is experienced, and will be remembered, as an affront to their personal worth, this being the price to pay for the single-minded pursuit of academic excellence with bright pupils?

Of course, the dichotomy is a false one. Many schools are already using techniques which help each child to maximise his intellectual potential and enhance his sense of self-worth. These techniques involve a broadening of classroom objectives to include development areas across the full range of the individual pupil's talent. Figures 1.2 and 1.3 give some indication of just how complex adolescent potential is and, in operating a pastoral-sensitive curriculum at classroom level all these developmental potentials need to be borne in mind. Problems have arisen when schools have concentrated exclusively on one developmental area, perhaps the cognitive area (column C, Figure 1.3) or the socio-emotional area (column A, Figure 1.3). Each is important but none can be the exclusive concern of the school. Although psychologists have made logical, theoretical divisions, each area has a reciprocating effect on the others. Paul Nash (1968) comments:

> The human personality cannot be neatly dissevered in this way. If educators confine their attention to the intellectual development of their pupils they will find that their failure to regard the whole personality vitiates even their attempts at intellectual training ... Although these mundane details may be anathema to the 'pure' intellectual teacher, he ignores them at his pedagogical peril.

Nash continues by making the equally important observation, very significant from a guidance point of view, that:

> There is an additional reason why intellectual training is inadequate as a sole educational aim. Intellectual power and skill can be used toward evil ends as well as good ... It is indeed the disastrous attempt of some of the most educated, cultured, and intellectually disciplined nations in the world that has brought about a revival of the demand for an essential moral content in education.

From a practical point of view, then, how can a school set about the task of creating a pastorally sensitive curriculum? In working with teachers, I often find a wide degree of support for the position that academic and pastoral aims are congruent and mutually supportive. The problem which is regularly and forcefully presented is that while ethically and pedagogically a pastorally sensitive curriculum is desirable, from a practical point of view it is not possible. It would be foolish on my part to suggest that any structured curriculum change is easy, but I do suggest that a number of prior planning decisions will diminish the insolubility of the problem.

The crucial decision is that academic and pastoral teams should be integrated at the planning stage. The statement of Nash is forcefully echoed by the Inspectorate's paper (1977) on secondary curriculum planning:

> Most schools have found it necessary to set up a pastoral network, but only when all staff feel involved is the academic work effectively supported by this network. No pastoral system can function satisfactorily, divorced from the working life of the school.

If we accept that the human personality cannot be sliced into compartments, then no decisions about examinations, testing, vocational courses or remedial work should be taken without the involvement of, on the one hand, heads of academic departments and, on the other, heads of house, counsellors or other members of the guidance team. Equally, no policy decisions about the social, emotional, vocational or moral development of pupils should be taken without discussion by the same broad team. Failure to engage in this consultation will neutralise the work of both teachers of subjects and pastoral care staff. However, a study of Best, Jarvis, and Ribbins (1977) pinpoints a reason why this consultation frequently fails to occur. Unfortunately, their findings suggest schools have used guidance in an opportunist way, rather than pursue sound educational objectives. They suggest that, as comprehensivisation and its attendant mergers progressed, two problems emerged. Former grammar school teachers were faced with a discipline problem of dimensions they had rarely encountered in their previous existence, and former secondary modern school staff found their career progress blocked by the graduates from the grammar schools in applications for promotion. Pastoral systems emerged, not to pursue the real educational potential of such systems, but to offer a new career structure to the less academic school staff, and to thrust the discipline problem firmly into their arms and out of the classroom. Typical British pragmatism or cynical opportunism? Whichever was the cause, the result was that guidance frequently got off to a poor start, yet initially it was proposed as a vital, integral element in the large comprehensive system.

The close consultation between academic and pastoral staff is facilitated by setting up a structure which involves regular contact between, and evaluation of, both areas of the school's work. The structure of the planning team is a prerequisite, but it is not sufficient in itself. In the final analysis staff attitudes are more important than school structures. The team needs to hammer out a consensus on the school's view of its academic and pastoral responsibilities.

Teacher's attitudes

I was recently asked to run some workshop sessions in a large comprehensive school, which were designed to draw attention to the pastoral responsibilities of the subject departments. I saw my task as that of mere referee or holder of coats, since the designated task had to be an area where individual schools keep firm hold of responsibility for their decisions. I set up group sessions and tried to get both 'sides' (academics and pastorals) to delve deeper than the conventional courtesies which usually characterise debate about this fundamental issue. We unearthed an enormous amount of mutual hostility. Language was strong, positions aggressively stated, motives questioned, but by the end of our sessions a real understanding of each other's position was beginning to emerge. Should a school decide to tackle this problem of integration, it is well worth while employing the services of an outside group leader to help teachers probe critically and honestly the underlying attitudes which govern their performance. Surprisingly, industry and commerce have long recognised and used the potential of group psychology in developing productive team approaches, yet education soldiers on with its personnel often heaving in quite opposite directions.

The importance of teacher attitudes is argued by an increasing number of psychologists in their investigation of 'self-fulfilling prophecy'. Some 80 studies since 1965 strongly suggest that the teacher's expectation of what a pupil can do will affect what in fact the pupil does achieve. Probably the best summary of work so far is by Insel and Jacobson (1977).

M T Taylor (1976) analysed teachers' perceptions of their pupils and discovered that 50 per cent of the 'cognitive space' for judging children in the teachers he used was occupied by academic criteria. There are many reasons why this might be so (our own interests and values, our historical function, the correlation between academic factors and sociability factors) but the important point is that we tend to view our pupils as academic fodder – able or not able to succeed – and they respond accordingly.

It must be stated unequivocally that no teacher can claim to teach only his subject. He may want to, but he is incapable psychologically of doing simply that – even a teaching machine can produce anger, frustration, inadequacy and delight in a pupil. Many of us may have our interests primarily in a subject area, and that interest should be used in the most effective way possible with academically able children. But there must always be an acceptance and evaluation of this fact – that teaching activity consistently has socio-emotional effects on the pupils.

The Inspectorate's working paper on curriculum (1977) insists on the reciprocating effect of academic and social objectives. Few teachers would find any problem in accepting the consequences of that analysis and those who do, in the interests of the pupils, ought to discuss their reservations openly, honestly and courteously in a staff forum, so that a working consensus and some degree of congruence of aims can be achieved. The teacher who sees his work in academic terms only implicitly devalues those pupils whose academic skills are limited – they must either learn from him to lower their sense of personal worth or reject him as unworthy of attention. The debate is not about excellence and standards, it is about the individual dignity of human beings and the key nature of the relationship between pupil and teacher.

The pastorally sensitive curriculum – some examples

Since every teaching situation is unique, there must be some reluctance about offering suggested answers to another person's problems. The following outlines are offered as nothing more than thought-provokers, points of departure and springboards. Each teacher responds to his own teaching milieu in his own way.

A WHOLE SCHOOL APPROACH

One of the interesting curriculum experiments I observed in the United States had the unpromising name of 'morning exercise'. It appeared on the school timetable as a twice weekly, one-hour block for all classes at the same time, 10 am to 11 am. It was far from the mass callisthenics the title might lead one to expect.

Aim

The exercise was intended to help create and maintain mutual respect among teachers, pupils and ancillary staff.

It tried to give value to a broader range of talents than would normally appear in the classroom.

It gave the opportunity for staff to see pupils more roundly, and for pupils to see staff more roundly.

It gave the opportunity for all pupils to develop self-confidence. It shared the responsibility of 'content' with the pupils.

Organisation

The school drama department was responsible for organising this part of the timetable. Everyone in the school – teachers, pupils and ancillary staff – knew that as individuals or groups they could ask for a time slot on the programme; the length varied from as little as one minute to a quarter of an hour. That time would be used by the person who requested it as he wished – to recite a poem, to make a speech (often critical of the school), to play a guitar, sing, dance or act. The range was enormous, taste was catholic and a tradition of courteousness in response well established. The principle seemed to be: if this is important to the performer, let's give him a chance.

A fiery black girl read some militant poems she had written, deploying swearwords like land mines to shock the establishment. She was applauded politely at the end. That reaction, I suppose, made it possible for an elderly head of department to appear one day and say, 'I would like to share with you the Lord's Prayer'. He was listened to in respectful silence – because everyone else had been.

Evaluation

The cohesive effect on the whole school was remarkable. Obviously, there were problems – largely the problem of pupils swearing in poems. That seemed a small price to pay, as the most unlikely characters dazzled with displays of virtuosity in the most esoteric of arts.

Adaptability

The principles of this exercise can be used at all levels – whole school, house, year-group and individual classroom. Academic objectives were pursued when children in a small group chose to dramatise an incident from a set book or hold a debate on some issue.

On odd occasions the whole hour was given over to one group – one of the most memorable was when the girls did a one-hour fashion parade on ethnic styles. Since the school had blacks, Puerto-Ricans, Japanese and Chinese, the interest and expertise were high.

SEVERAL CLASSES TOGETHER

'Group reading' was an attempt by an urban high school to integrate academic and pastoral objectives in the classroom.

Aim

To tackle the academic problem of introducing a mixed ability group to the concepts of plot, characterisation and theme in the novel.

To develop the pupils' skill in co-operative group work.

To develop attitudes of mutual respect and a sense of value of self in a group of children with mixed abilities.

To develop reading, analytic and critical skills.

Organisation

A group of 80 children whose ages ranged from 11 to 14 were invited to select one book from a series offered to them. Each book contained about 200 pages, and the list included authors like Steinbeck, Hemingway, Bradbury and Weisel. On the basis of the children's choice small groups were constructed – about 15 per group, with one teacher.

The first problem was to help slow readers complete the reading (the novels had been chosen because they were terse, largely concerned with plot) and this was tackled by the teacher reading aloud to a subgroup of poor readers, or by using taped recordings while the good readers worked through the book in a library period. This part of the exercise took about three weeks.

The discussion was structured so that everyone could participate. The teacher focused on the less able or younger children for less complex answers and the more capable children for more complex replies. I observed work on one such project with the Bradbury science fiction story, *The Blue Pyramid*. Simply, the story takes place in the future. A young couple await the birth of their first child and the mother-to-be delivers the child in a 'standard' pain-remover. After the birth, it is announced that unfortunately the baby has been transferred by the machine into a different dimension; to eyes accustomed to this dimension it appears to be a blue pyramid; to ears in this dimension, its cries are heard as whistling squeaks. The parents are faced with the dilemma of how to respond to their child – by rejecting it or accepting it.

All the children participated in outlining the plot. Then a brief exercise in character analysis began with the question, 'Who do you like best in the story?', with a following request for justification of the choice. Again there was full participation and an opportunity to discuss personal values and attitudes. The most difficult part was to try and look at the theme. The question, 'Why does an author write a story?' drew answers like 'to make money' and 'to entertain'. One child eventually said, 'If you have something special to say, you can tell it in a story.' This provided the starting point for a long discussion which lasted several class periods about the theme of the book – the special thing that Bradbury wanted to say.

The group eventually decided that the theme was a question: 'What are the fundamental qualities which make someone human?' And again the guidance possibilities of the curriculum were shown.

While this was going on, the other groups were reading and discussing their books, and the teachers had agreed that the final phase of the exercise would be an invitation to each group to 'present' its book to the others. There were dramatisations, television interviews of main characters, formal critical reviews and visual displays which illustrated the book. I was intrigued when my group decided on a simple ploy. They constructed an enormous blue pyramid out of coloured perspex and inside each group member placed examples of what he regarded as being quintessentially human.

Evaluation

I was particularly impressed by the full class participation – all the children contributed at all stages. The deliberate attempt to create a valuing atmosphere seemed to encourage contributions from the least able, and the clearly stated socio-emotional objectives seemed to have a positive effect on the eagerness with which the children pursued the academic concepts.

Adaptability

There is a growing body of research (collated by Abercrombie [1979]) which suggests that the social milieu of learning affects participation by group members and the effectiveness of their learning. The general approach outlined above – planning socio-emotional outcomes together with academic ones – presents the possibility of more effective learning in all subjects.

INDIVIDUAL CHILDREN

A scheme initiated by the county of Wiltshire tried to develop a method of publicly valuing pupil talent beyond (and in addition to) the academic. The experiment became known as the Swindon Record of Personal Achievement Scheme. It proposes that pupils personally complete a record of those activities they consider valuable and that the record be used, along with any examination results, to broaden the picture that we have of pupils. The Schools Council (1979) evaluation of the scheme comments that normally the picture of the child is 'thought of largely, if not exclusively, in terms of examination results'. The pamphlet continues that while examination results are 'invaluable as an alternative to nepotism, (they) probably should not be regarded as the total answer'. This movement has had a very strong influence on the development of profiling (see Chapter 4).

Aim

To provide information about non-examination pupils, and to increase their motivation.

To give supplementary information on examination pupils.

To provide indicators to teachers of pupil interests, thus helping in the task of appropriate teaching responses.

Organisation

In a loose-leaf folder pupils are asked to record their personal achievements. The decision on what is to be recorded is the child's and a supporting comment from an adult can be added. It is important that the quality of the folder be such that it can withstand normal classroom wear and retain an attractive appearance. (The average cost of an individual CSE entry was felt to be a useful measuring stick.)

Evaluation

A detailed description and evaluation of the scheme was published as Schools Council Pamphlet 16 which emphasises the enormous potential of the scheme, and suggests that greater training of teachers in its use would increase its benefits to the pupils. It concluded that what happened in Swindon was the beginning of a movement which would help to involve that group of pupils who are relatively unaffected by their final years in school.

Adaptability

There are numerous possibilities of varying the age group using the scheme, the method of filling in the folders, integrating the scheme into the curriculum, and involving parents and local employers. As always teacher commitment to the activity is essential for its success.

Summary

This chapter has argued that for any teacher to attempt to opt out of the pastoral dimension of his responsibility borders on the unprofessional. The most important method of giving pastoral care to pupils and of enhancing their personal growth cannot occur in a parallel pastoral system. It occurs centrally in and through the everyday lessons of the school.

Chapter 2
Healthy Classrooms

Teachers in Britain have a long tradition of concern for the personal welfare of their pupils which contrasts strongly with other more formal education systems. The previous chapter suggests that this was not merely a philosophical statement about the intrinsic value of human beings, but a shrewd (though probably not conscious) awareness that personal, social and emotional well-being is the most fertile ambience within which to pursue more conventional school activities. Children, like plants, need sunshine to grow. How surprising, then, to find myself writing on school-generated disruptive behaviour in this way: 'If a group of psychologists, expert in attitude formation, were invited to devise a situation and create a series of experiences specifically to provoke young people into disruptive, hostile or aggressive behaviour, they could well come up with something uncomfortably close to what is experienced by large numbers of pupils in many British secondary schools.' (McGuiness and Craggs, 1986) How can it be that an organisation whose task is to enhance the potential and develop the talent of young people can in some cases stunt that growth, leaving the youngsters bewildered, resentful and hostile towards the source of their frustration?

The solution to the paradox lies in the distinction made in the previous chapter between *task* and *social* concern. When the school (or the individual teacher) reduces consideration of personal and social development of pupils to mere rhetoric, the pursuit of all other aims becomes fundamentally flawed. In a very real sense, the teacher who sets socio-emotional considerations on one side is building on sand. Not only is the effectiveness of the task-pursuit diminished, but the pupils are also sold short on personal development on what the Inspectorate (1979, p 206) has called 'the central purpose of education'.

Until recently, self theory (Burns 1982, 1979; Thomas 1973; Snygg and Combs 1959; Rogers 1962, 1969, 1983) has had a very limited influence on pedagogy in British schools. Yet if, as Snygg and Combs suggest, the maintenance and enhancement of self-esteem is 'the all-inclusive human need which motivates all behaviour, at all times, in all places', it must be argued that it merits central consideration. Self-esteem, our ability to see ourselves as possessed of intrinsic, inviolable dignity, a sense of personal worth, is used as a major construct of mental health. It has been suggested that when our self-esteem is attacked our defence of it is virtually a reflex action. Such an attack has been compared to having one's supply of air cut off – the desperate battle to get air is paralleled psychologically by the ferocity and tenacity with which we defend our self-esteem. Most of us will be able to recall an occasion when we were publicly devalued – and to relive the fierce, self-protective surge of indignation which followed. The implications for the classrooms are obvious. As a language teacher, the *first* evaluative question I need to ask is not 'Do they now understand the difference between the perfect and imperfect tenses?' but rather 'Was my classroom a safe place for the self-esteem of these pupils?' If the answer is negative, all the evidence suggests that the pupils' main consideration in the classroom will have been protecting their self-esteem. Not to give very serious attention to the effect of my teaching on pupil self-esteem will inevitably lead to under-performance by pupils.

Some years ago, counselling a student in my university, I was having unusual difficulty in helping her to talk. Eventually, I asked this young woman to fill in four 'bubbles' I had drawn in comic form around her name (Figure 2.1). She filled the bubbles in in a surprising way given that she was a very attractive, intelligent young woman. Where had that view of her self come from? Was she fishing for compliments? The heartbroken sobs suggested that the vision of herself was all too real.

Most of us in our early childhood are treated in a way that allows us to build up reserves of self-esteem. Our parents, siblings and wider family give us constant messages that we are lovable, talented, worth cuddling, even when we have been naughty. We see ourselves as having worth. Of course, some children, like Mary, receive different messages and emerge from childhood quite severely damaged. The vast majority are psychologically caressed and cuddled in a way that enhances mental health. How does that happen?

We all form two important mental constructs in the various situations in which we find ourselves. Thus in childhood, at home, we form a *self-image*, a picture of ourselves, an answer to the question, who am I? I bring home a painting from playgroup. 'Oh, that's beautiful!' says Mum, 'Is it bonfire night?' 'No,' replies the child,

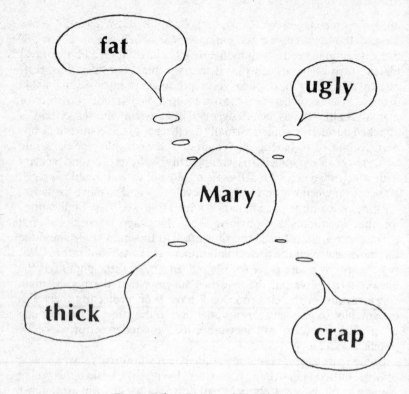

Figure 2.1. *A 20-year-old's self-image*

reproachfully, 'It's grandad.' 'Oh, yes, I see – it's lovely. We must show it to him.' And so it goes on. The child learns about his talent, that he is worthy of attention. Grandad will reinforce that when he pins the picture up in his kitchen.

At the same time the child learns about the kind of person who is especially admired in his home. He learns that kind people, helpful people, good readers, hard-working people are admired – he is forming what the jargon tells us is an *ideal self*. Such admired people are seen as worthy of imitations, criteria against which to measure our own worth. Thus the child will lay his growing self-image alongside the ideal self presented to him by his environment and, to the extent to which he finds they match, will emerge with a sense of personal worth, or self-esteem (Figure 2.2).

The issue is not, in a real sense, moral. People can establish self-esteem on the basis of behaviours that are objectively not moral. Some

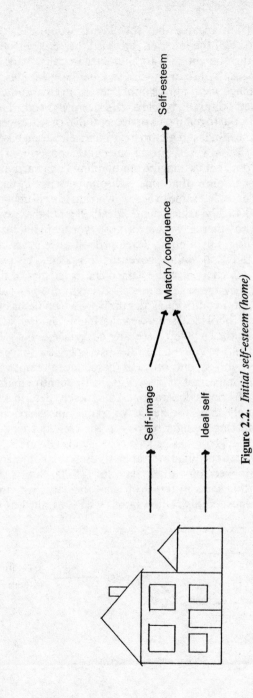

Figure 2.2. *Initial self-esteem (home)*

years ago, a student from an area that sociologists would call 'the delinquescent sub-culture of the inner city' regaled the class with the story of how his mother taught him to shop-lift. Initially, bars of chocolate, then giant packets of soap powder, graduating eventually to duffle coats! His self-image was 'I am a skilful thief' in an environment that admired and valued skilful thieves. His self-esteem was high. This is not to defend thieving, but to remind us of the centrality of self-esteem in maintaining mental health. Is it better to have high self-esteem based on antisocial activity, or low self-esteem in genteel poverty? The question is not an idle one. Let us imagine our budding Fagan arriving at school. We all exist in more than one environment, and in each environment we experience that same process – who am I? (self-image). What kind of person is highly valued here? (ideal self). Do these two constructs match in a way that leaves me feeling a worthy individual?

So the skilful shop-lifter, full of home-developed self-esteem, arrives at school. Like many pupils, he will discover that his talents, his self-image, are difficult to match against the valued characteristics of the school. He may pick up new messages in the school environment – I am stupid, non-academic, non-conforming, disruptive – which he has to attempt to match to the school ideal self – we value highly children who are conforming academics. Unable to see any congruence, his self-esteem becomes difficult to maintain, the psychological oxygen essential for mental health is cut off. His desperate attempts to maintain that essential component of his well-being frequently emerge as disruption, truancy or non-cooperation. This merely describes a process – it is certainly not a defence or pupil misbehaviour. Nevertheless, it is a sobering thought to look at the consequences of failure to put self-esteem high on our pedagogical agenda (Figure 2.3).

The young people who fit the Figure 2.3 analysis drew this comment: 'These children are invited day after day for 15,000 hours to contemplate their worthlessness in terms of what their teachers and school evidently prize most highly. Those pupils who learn the lesson

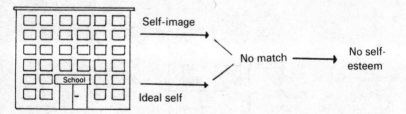

Figure 2.3. *School and self-esteem*

of docility must carry away from school an indelible impression of their inadequacy and inferiority. Others, who have a more resilient attachment to their sense of personal worth, reject school as an inauthentic commentator on their personal worth, by truancy or disruption – these we label deviant.' (McGuiness [1983], p 178)

It is a strange paradox that those children who roundly declare a commitment to an integral part of their well-being are seen as deviant. The task of the teacher seeking to create a healthy classroom is to ensure high levels of positive feedback for the pupils' self-image, and to broaden the range of qualities valued in the school-projected ideal self. That really does mean the languages and the physics teachers, the mathematicians and the geographers allowing their interaction with pupils to spill far beyond the conventional academic boundaries into the social and emotional realities of the class. This needs to be done deliberately, constructively and creatively, just like academic planning, since doing no planning is not neutral in its outcome – it is counter-productive. The teacher who does not plan his academic work has a negative effect on pupils' academic development. No less, the teacher who fails to scrutinise with the same professionalism the socio-emotional outcomes of his work will damage pupils in an area central to their well-being.

It is important to state clearly that I am not advocating a lowering of standards, a dilution of our educational aims. Quite the contrary – I am proposing that a professional analysis of classroom practice will reveal that an almost obsessional concern for academic success has been counter-productive by destroying the foundation on which that success is built.

It is understandable that 'subjects' are intrinsically justified and are seen as served by personal education – after all, schools exist to maximise our young people's academic talent. However, understandable though it may be, it is more difficult to justify in terms of research. It is very difficult to find any research which establishes a clear relationship between academic success and later success in life. Indeed, several researchers find that such a relationship does not exist. The previous chapter mentioned that Kohlberg (1977), Heath (1977) and Nicholson (1970), all carried out investigations independently and in different places and could find no independent correlation between scholastic aptitude in pupils and later life success. Their reports (respectively) that 'school academic achievement made no independent contribution to successful life adjustment', that 'scholastic aptitude was not related to life success' and that 'academic achievement was not significantly related to a broad and multiple definition of life success' must make even the most die-hard academic pause. The researchers were not saying that clever children did not make it in life, but they were saying that clever children would make it *only if certain other socio-emotional characteristics* had been developed. Equally, they do not propose the pursuit of low academic standards, but they do argue forcefully that those children who lack strong academic ability will still make it if those same socio-emotional features have been worked on. They discovered two consistent and independent correlates with a child's ability to become a successful adult. Those children who at school have developed a) social skill and confidence, and b) a powerful sense of personal worth, will turn out to be successful adults in significantly large proportions. Thus, the key finding is that the most precious gift we can give to our pupils is not academic prowess (important though that is), it is that essential self-esteem and the ability to operate confidently in a variety of social contexts. Conversely, those teachers who fail to work on these areas, or worse, who actually damage that aspect of a child's development, are doing life-long harm of incalculable consequence. In addition to the research cited, Coopersmith (1967), Briggs (1970), Samuels (1977) and Borba and Borba (1978) are impressive contributors to a wide range of educators who subscribe to the Borbas' view – 'a positive, self-enhancing atmosphere is essential to a child's educational success' (1978).

It is, then, increasingly clear that as teachers we need to enhance our ability to respond to children's socio-emotional growth, as well as honing our academic skills. The following chapter will examine in detail how that might be achieved in practice. Suffice it to say at the moment that it is not sufficient to concentrate on skills; the *person* of the teacher is an influence of inestimable significance in classroom interaction. The question is not only 'What do I need to *do* in this encounter?' but 'What kind of a person do I need to be?'

The slow journey towards recognition that relationships within the school are the key to healthy classrooms, and that the teacher being able to *be* himself rather than a role is the key to these relationships, has taken place alongside a developing view of pastoral care. The initial *ad hoc*, liberal valuing of pupils as individuals, inherited from the public schools and grammar schools, soon ran into trouble in the new comprehensive schools. Best, Jarvis and Ribbins (1977) perceptively outline the way in which the new, all-ability co-educational schools presented staff with two related, counterpointing challenges. The former staff of the old grammar schools were suddenly faced with levels of low motivation and ill-discipline that contrasted unpleasantly with the disposition of most of their former pupils. Having worked all their professional lives with a carefully selected, most able 20 per cent, they now faced a genuine full-ability range. I was one of those teachers. It was a chastening experience. My previous discussions of synonym with a couple of Oxbridge-bound students of Russian were light years away from the work I now had to do with non-examination classes. I had to re-learn my professional skills, look again at the nature of teaching.

At the same time, highly talented colleagues, who had been teaching in secondary modern schools with great success, now found their career opportunities blocked, often by younger but better qualified (academically) former grammar school staff. The opportunistic (might one say, cynical) solution to both problems was to establish a pastoral system (originally intended to be an integral part of the new, all-ability schools) which was a 'sin-bin' to which the disruptive, slow-learning group could be consigned, and a structure with a career ladder for displaced 'non-academic' staff. The administrative elegance of this pseudo-solution blinded us all to the fact that we had subverted pastoral care in a fundamental way. It had been separated from the academic life of the school and it had been devalued into a haven for less qualified staff and less able pupils. The central purpose of education was to be pursued in a safety net.

We are still wrestling with that perception of pastoral care but we are winning (Figure 2.4). Very quickly, teachers saw the inadequacy of the safety net approach. The immense social changes of the 1960s and 1970s led to a demand for new materials which took a more developmental view of children's personal development. We demanded and received new materials and approaches, and they began to pour into schools. Developmental group work, active tutorial work, experiential learning packs, carefully prepared syllabuses from the Schools Council, Baldwin, Wells, Hopson, Scally, Button, Priestly,

Whole school approach

Full integration,
developmental focus

Special pastoral curriculum

Minimal integration, but
developmental focus

Safety net

Separate, parallel
systems.
Reactive, crisis
focus

Figure 2.4. *Development of pastoral care*

McGuire and many others became available as offerings for a 'pastoral curriculum'. Schools inserted 'tutorial' periods, life and social skills lessons or personal and social education slots into their timetables with varying degrees of success. The authors of the excellent materials had warned that their use involved *radically new pedagogical approaches*, yet some schools tried to use essentially collaborative, experiential learning material in the old, teacher-centred academic model. Again, we had failed to see that, useful though the new materials were, they failed to address the key issue. If children were being damaged by an inappropriate curriculum, a 'supplementary vitamins' approach was almost as inadequate as the safety net approach. Both undoubtedly help, but neither tackles the problem at its root. A teaching colleague at an INSET meeting put her finger on it for me. 'I've just realised,' she said, 'PSE is simply a supplement for our bad teaching in the ordinary curriculum.'

That slightly exaggerates the case. Nevertheless, just as the safety net approach, with its crisis focus and reactive approach, contained an inherent acceptance of a damaging curriculum, so the 'special' pastoral curriculum leaves some children puzzled by the fact that in the tutorial period they are valued, collaborative, involved and active, while in their academic subjects they can be under-valued, passive recipients of examination material. In that sense, as my teaching colleague had said, we have used our pastoral periods to supplement bad teaching.

However, my experience in the late 1980s is that a strong move towards whole school approaches is under way. Lang's excellent (1988) initiative on primary school pastoral care reminds us of the initial integrative and permeative approach to personal development of pupils in primary schools. The enhancement of pupils' esteem, the development of their social confidence and skills is increasingly tackled in the French, maths, geography, chemistry etc, lessons. This move to a whole school approach to pastoral care is, of course, inevitable. It does take time, as we learn to view our academic activity more wholly, and while we move down that integrated road, we will maintain the old approaches like vestigial organs in some evolutionary process – organs that increasingly fall into disuse (Figure 2.5).

We need each of these approaches, but the better we are in our whole school approach, the less we will need the 'supplementary' and 'safety net' approaches.

The consequences of adopting a whole school approach to pastoral care is that all teachers become responsible for it. The personal development of pupils is pursued in a professional, deliberate way by each member of staff. There can be no opting out.

Developmental

Crisis management
(Safety net)

Involves *some* staff.
Focus on 'deficient' pupils.
Focus on *problems*
eg Discipline
Motivation
Domestic issues
Divorce
Parental imprisonment
Bereavement
Child abuse

Pastoral curriculum
(Supplementary)

Involves *some* staff.
Develops specific aims.
Focus on pupils
eg Active tutorial work
Developmental group work
Careers work
Esteem enhancement
Decision-making skills

Whole school approaches

Involves *all* staff.
Uses *whole* curriculum to pursue
socio-emotional development of
pupils.
Concern with school and classroom
climate as *main delivering system of
pastoral care*

Figure 2.5. *Pastoral realities of our schools*

Summary

The key to a whole school approach to pastoral care, which has been argued in the opening chapter, lies in the creation of healthy classrooms. Though understandable, it is no longer adequate to use 'safety net' or 'supplementary' approaches to the personal development of our pupils.

Chapter 3

The Professionals

So far, I have tried to argue that the safety net view of pastoral care is an untenable separation of the content and process of learning. Both the social climate of the learning situation and the specific tasks pursued by the learners must be prepared for and implemented together, if they are not reciprocally to damage each other's effects – academic aims single-mindedly pursued, destroying crucial self-esteem, socio-emotional aims failing to accept the academic responsibilities of the school. They are cement and bricks, intimately and essentially partners. Further, I would argue that the supplementary view of pastoral care as specialist input, while currently necessary, is a regrettable recognition that our academic teaching is diminished by our failure to subject the full dynamics of the classroom to professional scrutiny. As one school colleague said recently, 'Separate personal and social education is nothing more than a supplement to reduce the effects of inadequate classroom teaching.' The objectives of the 'pastoral curriculum' should be included among the objectives of the subject specialists, not only to integrate pastoral care, but also because such integration will enhance the quality of academic teaching.

Of course, most teachers received minimal initial training in the discharge of their socio-emotional responsibilities. Those considerations were seen as an incidental spin-off of the personality of the teacher. But given the central effects that this area of teaching has on children's development, such a cavalier approach is at best risky and at worst unforgivably unprofessional. Teachers were aware of this and as the 1970s moved into the 1980s, these neglected constructs began to be included in curriculum planning. Teachers demanded a new range of materials to respond to the demands of structural unemployment, increased discretionary time, the demands of the post-industrial society. A vast range of pedagogical aids and packs appeared on the market – excellent materials invariably accompanied by a caveat that these new process-focused materials required new pedagogical skills from teachers: negotiating goals, methods and appraisal, using experiential methods, understanding and using the dynamics of groups. INSET courses sprang up to meet the training demand and many schools are reaping the benefit of these courses. We are, of course, only halfway there, in the sense that the most carefully nurtured skills can be subverted if they are bolted on to inadequately examined personal feelings, values and attitudes. The real 'me' is an infallibly accurate indicator-filter through which all our skills will be mediated to the pupil. In 1988, writing on counselling and special educational need, I made the point this way (Figure 3.1).

1	2	3	4	5
The teacher in role $\rightarrow$	Intent/ task/goal $\rightarrow$	Skills/ techniques necessary $\rightarrow$	'Real me' feelings/ attitudes/ values $\rightarrow$	Pupil

Figure 3.1. *Teacher to pupil – with feeling*

This linear representation is one way of viewing practice, and in our initial training and professional development it is (4) which is commonly left unexamined. It is the old error, even in the area of social *skill*, of concentrating on task. There is something deeper than skill which infuses for good or ill all our relationships. McGuiness and Gilliland (1988) put it thus:

> We relate to our pupils by means of a complex of skills which may or may not be compatible with the deeper view of ourselves. For example, what exchange with a pupil (5) could possibly grow from an INSET programme designed to develop participatory learning strategies (3) in someone who is profoundly authoritarian (4)? Or how could someone work wholeheartedly with an epileptic pupil (5), despite a course in first-aid skills (3), if the person is fearful of physical convulsions (4)? Or again, how would a teacher (1) relate to a sexually abused pupil (5) if their own response to sexuality is ambiguous or unexamined (4)? The important point is that between the teacher and the pupil lies the 'real me' of the teacher – it must be a 'me' of which the teacher is aware if a fully professional analysis of teacher effect is to occur. It is the same old question – in teaching, we need first to ask not 'what do I have to *do* here?', but 'who do I have to *be* here?'

It is a very hard question to put on to the agenda, but it is, as all the psychological evidence indicates, the real professional question.

For some years I have been involved in counsellor training and have observed how nurses, general practitioners, industrial and commercial managers, the armed services, the police and teachers came to the courses, not to become counsellors but to enhance their relationship ability in the expectation that in some sense their 'performance' will be helped. There is, then, a growing realisation, even among the cost-conscious members of the business world that to get in touch with the real me is not some wishy-washy self-indulgence, but an analysis of a powerful influence on performance in a wide range of activities. The professionals must be listened to.

Part of our counsellor-training course involves one hour per week of a group exercise called sensitivity training. This is an opportunity for a group of 12 people to explore themselves (their 'real me') and their relationship with others in the group to a depth and with an honesty not frequently possible. It is an opportunity, an invitation. There is, one fervently hopes, total freedom to share only at the level at which each member feels comfortable. The technique is well described in the literature (Rogers, 1971; Blomberg and Golembiewski, 1976). At the opening session, and periodically during the year, privacy is identified as a prized value. We resist, as a group, uninvited intrusion or pressure to disclose beyond the point at which an individual feels comfortable. In our task (to stand close to our self) the social climate of the group has to be safe. The pace at which each group progresses, the issues raised, the interactions shared are very much group-specific, but certain general issues arise regularly. Because the group is 'leaderless' in the sense that it is invited to take responsibility for its own development, there is an initial disorientation. Who am I, here? Usually in group situations there are clear markers of authority and responsibility – with a strong task focus. Here the task is coming to terms with self, the potential for initiative and/or opting out, resisting and/or sabotage are total. Thus authority is soon on the agenda – a central issue for teachers, as was suggested in the example of the 'authoritarian' trained in participatory learning methods. In time, all the strong influences on our ways of relating emerge – fear, betrayal, loyalty, trust, encourage-ment, support, blocking ourselves, blocking others, sexuality, anger, and so on. Classrooms are full of these influences and to respond in something more sophisticated than an unconscious, knee-jerk way involves the hard work of coming to terms with self. Though they have clear professional consequences, the matters raised are very private, and so a careful balance needs to be maintained between the valuing of privacy in all the interactions and the willingness of participants to monitor at a personal level those areas that are particularly sensitive. It requires that scrupulously honest analysis which is the hallmark of professionalism. It was very gratifying to hear one initial trainee teacher say, after a series of sensitivity training sessions, 'This is the first time in three years that I have been invited to consider myself ... but surely I must be a crucial factor in the classroom equation.'

One exercise sometimes used in sensitivity training illustrates the accuracy of that statement. Participants are invited to relax and draw to mind one of their parents, and to get as close as they can to that parent in their mind. They are asked to see the world through the eyes of that parent, as far as possible to *be* that parent. Then each group member in turn is asked to speak for one minute in the role of their chosen parent. The topic for one minute is 'my child', ie they are invited to contemplate themselves through the eyes of their parent. It is a very powerful exercise – not to be used without trained leaders present – and it invariably releases much buried material, unresolved issues and not unusually tears. Such an exercise is only attempted when a high level of group cohesiveness and trust has been established and, even then, great care is taken to remind participants that the exercise is an invitation, not an obligation. On one occasion a participant (let's say Pat to choose a name that could apply to either sex) declined the invitation, saying, 'I'd find it too much; I'd rather just observe, if I may.' That was fine – we had emphasised the full freedom of individuals to disclose only as much as they felt was appropriate. The rest of the group completed the exercise and Pat said that being able to observe was 'a privilege' – at no point was any pressure exerted to gain any further disclosure.

Months later Pat came to see me saying, 'I think I ought to withdraw from the course.' I asked what the problem was and was told that during a counselling session with a volunteer client (all students produce a videotape of a counselling session as part of their assessed material), the client, recently bereaved, had begun to sob uncontrollably. The trainee counsellor told me that his/her response had been to try to put the lid firmly on this intense display of emotion – 'Don't cry, it'll be okay, you'll see. Time is a great healer.' The client had been refused permission to be herself. 'I realised,' said Pat, 'that I was not blocking her tears, but my own.'

I recalled the session months before when Pat had decided to observe. Pat remembered it and said the two things were related. I suggested that we could do the exercise now if Pat wanted to. The suggestion was accepted and Pat became the parent it was impossible to be several months earlier. The unresolved mourning, the blocked tears, the unfinished business, so influential yet so inaccessible earlier, were able to be shared and dealt with at this later stage. Pat is now using counsellor skills, but mediated through a self which has been honestly faced.

The point of that long anecdote is that the counsellor discovered something that all those involved in interpersonal helping relationships need to learn – that if we want to help other people (for us it is our pupils), if we want to be able to stand close by them as they face issues of fear, betrayal, loyalty, trust, encouragement, blocking, sexuality, anger and authority, we need to have learned to stand close to ourselves. Gerard Egan (1986) calls it 'coming to terms with the problematic in ourselves'. It is a task for teachers at least as much as for members of the medical profession, the social services, business and the armed and police services. Not to take that task on condemns our pupils to carrying the burden of *our* unfinished business. To help them answer the question 'who am I?', we need to have tackled it ourselves.

The person of the teacher, then, is of inestimable significance in classroom interaction, and a consequence of that reality is an acceptance that a central part of our professional development ought to focus on explaining what is the 'real me' through which our work with pupils is filtered. This lies at the heart of the next stage of developing pastoral care in our schools. As a colleague in a Liverpool comprehensive put it, 'Our pastoral care is now stuck until we all develop counselling ability.' Having escaped the safety net trap, we are locked into supplemental responses until we are *all* able to take on, in a fully professional manner, the interpersonal implications of the devolved pastoral role.

The specific role of counselling in school will be considered later in Chapter 6 but it is noteworthy that Rogers (1983) insists that the skills of the counsellor are, in a sense, the skills of any human relationship. The same qualities in a relationship that lead to successful outcomes in counselling are central to successful parent–child relationships, marital relationships, friendships – and teacher–pupil relationships. Counselling is a very complex concept but, in concentrating on the relationship element instead of the process and techniques, we can say that the counsellor tries to create the kind of relationship in which another person can feel sufficiently safe to explore self and take the risks involved in growing. It is not a bad description of what good teachers, the real professionals, have always done, building on sound relationships the courage to explore the unknown with their pupils. How is it to be done?

Of course, we need a high measure of academic competence ourselves. But the evidence overwhelmingly takes us back to the psychological prior need of a safe ambience if risks are to be taken. The ability to communicate that element of safety and support to pupils, then, is a major task of the teacher. Rogers (1965), Truax and Carkhuff (1967), and Carkhuff and Berenson (1977) have identified a number of what are called core conditions for effective relationships. They argue that when these conditions are absent, relationships will not encourage confidence and exploration; but when they are present, the individuals do gain the courage and awareness to face the most taxing challenges. In the language of one staffroom veteran, who had probably not heard of Truax or Carkhuff, 'The kids'll walk over live coals for Tom.' Tom, a teacher with highly developed relationships with his class, created the kind of feeling of security that had his pupils willing to explore the most difficult challenges. An observer would find the classrooms of teachers like Tom full of a number of qualities which analysts of the counselling process in the 1960s discovered were characteristics of successful counsellors.

Such teachers see their pupils as having inviolable dignity and treat them with respect. They see the difficulty of finding that core of dignity in some pupils but have had their faith sufficiently rewarded to make it unshakeable. They can distinguish the sinner from the sin, the bad behaviour from the misbehaver himself. Such respect is, of course, infectious, as is the opposite. Where children are treated with contempt, as not having dignity, they will resist the source of that contempt, precisely encapsulated in the phrase 'Kids don't learn from people they don't like.'

Further, the Toms of this world are able and willing to get into the skins of their pupils, to try to see the world with their perspective. It is a special gesture of respect, valuing the frame of reference of our pupils. Again, not to be able to do it establishes a distance, a remoteness which militates against creating the feelings of support and safety which underpin the courageous exploration we call learning.

Of enormous difficulty is the challenge to be genuine. Rogers calls it a willingness to be 'transparent' in the presence of our pupils. It is presenting the 'real me' instead of the role, a person instead of an office. A classroom where this does not occur has pretend relationships, since both parties rapidly learn not to be themselves. There is a pseudo-level of safety under which both parties grind through their lives in an emotional vacuum. In classrooms where I have seen a teacher risk being real, there is a richness and vibrancy that is almost tangible. I recall one 'difficult' class sitting spellbound in a poetry lesson when a teacher shared his experience of the birth of his child, and then went on to talk about feelings with the class. They shared as if their lives depended on it.

The ability to be concrete, 'immediacy' as the textbooks call it, is the final core condition of effective relationships identified by the researchers. It refers to that sensitivity which allows us to pick up tiny nuances of behaviour and to respond to them *as they occur*. 'That seems to make you feel a bit uneasy' you say as the ghost of a frown passes over a face. 'I can see a lot of you enjoying that' as a response to the gleaming eyes in the class. It is a response to the 'real me' of each pupil, changing the classroom from a precise minuet in which everyone has a pre-arranged role into a microcosm of the richness of our own and our pupils' lives.

So the healthy classroom is safe; it enhances and cherishes the self-esteem of all its occupants; it is full of respect and the ability to see the world through each other's eyes; it is genuine and without facade, and willing to face up to the reality of its interactions as they happen. Sadly, in those classrooms which are characterised by danger, by diminution of essential self-esteem, by contempt and narrow perspectives and by a denial of the reality of the interactions going on in it, both children and teachers are being damaged.

It is important to add two final comments to this chapter. We cannot regard classrooms dichotomously, as either healthy or unhealthy, though for the sake of drama and challenge I have tended to write in that stark way. It is important for us, nevertheless, to be aware of the polarity between those two end points, to identify where we are, and to ensure that there is a continual scrutiny of both our position and the direction of our movement. As I made clear in the opening comments of this book, the profession is profoundly aware of these issues, and moving strongly towards the healthy pole.

Nor should we treat ourselves as any less worthy of supportive relationships than our pupils. The challenge of new pedagogy and its implications for our style in the classroom are profound. Some of us will move in seven league boots, others by millimetres or even imperceptibly. All our colleagues will grow only when the atmosphere in which they work is full of respect, willingness to accept their perspectives, openness and immediacy. We need to feel safe if we are to grow too.

An exercise

I have found it useful, and my students tell me that they have got a great deal from it too, to spend five or ten minutes working alone in the class, writing down 'five bits of me that make it hard for other people to get on with me'. When everyone has done this, *invite* the group, working in groups of four, to share those qualities which they feel willing to share. It invites a level of openness and genuineness which is often very cohesive in its effect on the group. Then invite them to do the same exercise, only this time identifying five qualities which 'make it easier for people to get on with me'. Again, share as appropriate in groups of four. Surprisingly, saying nice things about ourselves is hard but again it knits the group together. It *is* important that the teacher does the exercise too, and the pupils *always* know if we are just going through the motions.

Summary

The professional teacher is willing to plan, monitor, evaluate and refine carefully *all* the consequences of his teaching. His mode of self-presentation will have a crucial effect on the way his pupils respond to the invitation to learn. Our colleagues in industry and commerce are very aware of the influence of the self on task performance.

Chapter 4
Testing Times

Despite the argument in the previous chapters that pastoral care is most effective when it focuses on problem prevention and pupil development, it will always be the case that, however carefully constructed the curriculum may be, there will remain a number of children with specific, marked difficulties in coping with school life. We can reduce the number of such children with 'preventive' approaches, but various studies suggest that at any one time about one-sixth of our children require some special educational response beyond that provided by the ordinary curriculum (Warnock, 1978).

If help is to be given to the child in difficulties, a system needs to be devised which regularly reviews each pupil in the school as an individual. To do this in a school of 1500 pupils, each of whom sees about eight different teachers weekly, can unfortunately no longer be left to chance encounter and personal contact. B M Moore (1970) suggested that a vital aspect of any guidance system must be a highly developed capacity for individualising pupils and, if this is to occur in large organizations, it must be planned.

Item 1 of Figure 4.1 presents as a general aim of guidance, appropriate for all schools, that staff should 'know and be able to individualise each pupil in the school'. The figure refines that general aim to two specific aims, one of which deals with the *accumulation* of information, knowledge, and data on pupils; the other highlights the need, in large schools with mobile staff and pupil population, of a cumulative *record system* which will give an element of continuity and stability to the data gathering. This chapter will tackle how a school might begin the first stage of that first general aim. A school should be able to answer with great accuracy the question 'Who are our pupils?'

As a class teacher with about 30 children in my group, I often became aware of how two or three of my pupils, on occasion, sank from view. There was no visible indication that this had happened; it was simply

General aims (all schools)	Specific aims	Strategies/techniques	Evaluative criteria
		These itemise available techniques used by some schools; appropriateness in a specific school must be carefully weighed by the staff	The important factor in monitoring a pastoral system is to seek behavioural outcomes related to the aims as evidence of success or failure. Again these will vary from school to school; but evaluative activity must occur if a pastoral system is to justify its existence
1. To know and be able to individualise each pupil in the school, thus providing a sound database for educational decision-making	1. (a) To locate problems early, eg underachievement, lack of coping skills, bullying, vandalism, truancy, bereavement, depression, disruption of classes, vocational confusion	1. (a) *Formal* – objective tests, school tests, case conferences, timetabled periods for guidance, contacts with parents, sociometry *Informal* – contact with pupils in sport, drama, field trips, lunch/ recreation, corridor observation, school parties	1. What is my school's data source? Is the information recorded factually? Is the system accessible and confidential? Are problems located early? Do pupils see themselves as individualised? Do staff know all the pupils?
	(b) To establish a factual, accessible, confidential system of records to give continuity to the attempt to individualise pupils	(b) Involvement of all staff in establishing and maintaining record system. Systematised entries	

Figure 4.1. *Knowing our pupils*

a sudden awareness that, although Bob was sitting in my class, my awareness of him was nil. In response to this (and conversations with other teachers suggest that this was not confined to my experience), I developed a personal strategy of deliberately establishing eye contact, touching, talking to, or listening to each child in the class in each lesson. The occasions in the staffroom when I was faced with the question 'Is Billy Barr at school?' and had to answer 'I don't know' (later to discover I had just taught him) disappeared.

At school level, the two or three who can sink from view can be 200 or 300. The consequent anonymity provides little motivation to sample what school has to offer, and can provide a shield for disturbed, withdrawn or malicious behaviour.

For example, Gary was 17 years old, timid, socially awkward, but academically able. He was a pupil in the lower sixth of a large urban comprehensive school. A police visit to the school, shortly after a Christmas holiday, revealed the following. A police patrol car had discovered Gary and his mother huddled together on a gravestone in the huge city cemetery, after residents had complained about the wailing coming from it in the early hours of the morning. The subsequent investigation showed that Gary and his mother had been brutally beaten by the father for many years, and that they had regularly sought refuge in the house of the mother's father. He had recently died, hence their bizarre and forlorn search for comfort by his grave on the occasion of the next attack. Gary's school had a well-established pastoral system which was totally unaware of the problem. He had remained a needle in the haystack.

Barbara (14, cocky, pretty and of average ability) was regarded as disruptive but not malicious. One Monday morning she astonished her maths teacher, who had reprimanded her failure to bring the necessary books by retorting 'You f---ing pig!' She burst into tears and ran out of the room. The school never discovered what emerged at the youth club later that night. The previous Sunday Barabara had been told by her mother that her 22-year-old brother, whom she adored, had been killed in Northern Ireland. 'Don't tell them pigs,' she warned the youth leader. 'They don't give a damn.' The 'pigs' were caring, concerned teachers, over-burdened with large classes, heavy timetables and the control problems of an inner-city school, who in addition had failed to extract this needle from the comprehensive haystack.

The examples are endless, and all experienced teachers can add their own harrowing examples; the child suicide, the terrorised pupil and, more recently, the child who doused himself with paraffin and set fire to himself. Inside each school can be hidden the truant, the school phobic, the bully and his victim, the slow learner, the dyslexic, the sexually assaulted, the vandal, the drug-taker, and the pregnant – children with difficulties, under stress, a threat to themselves or to others. Despite an understandably strong temptation to leave these complex problems hidden, failure to recognise them can have a destructive effect on the life of the whole school and disastrous results for the child in question.

Inevitably, we must face the paradox that our increasingly sophisticated diagnostic talents simply expose more problems and create more work for an unfairly over-burdened profession, and that the work required is in areas where teachers have little training. We can observe children meticulously, record assiduously and discover that in addition to the burdens of a normal curriculum, we need to empathise with a bereaved child, refer a battered child, counsel a pregnant child and support a depressed child. Few teachers would deny that from an ethical and professional point of view they had responsibilities in these areas; their disclaimers would be on the grounds of feasibility. At a recent INSET conference with teachers, as a group of 50 representative professionals, a quarter of an hour was spent collecting the types of specially challenging children the teachers had had to deal with during their careers. They identified well over 100 types of social, emotional, physical and intellectual challenges that we face as a profession, in addition to the normal challenge of academic teaching.

The practicability of a wider involvement with pupils is a major difficulty. The pedagogical load of pupil-centred approaches in TVEI and GCSE is seriously underestimated by administrators. The desperate, national search for maths teachers goes on in a context where one such teacher already in the profession can speak thus: 'I had 28 pupils in my class – five really very naughty, two quite disturbed. These two began to insult a sexually abused girl who is badly dressed and dirty. A kindly child in the class who has slight perinatal brain damage comes to her rescue, and for his pains becomes the object of the insults. He tries to run out of the room and school to where I know (lunch-time information) a motorcycle gang is waiting for another member of the class.' This superb teacher dealt with that incredibly complex managerial problem *and taught maths*.

At a national level, the professional associations of teachers must continue to demand from Government the kinds of staffing levels and resourcing which will allow schools to respond to the vastly more complex task that society has now assigned to them. The in-service training of teachers recommended so long ago in the James Report (1972) is not a perk, but a vital necessity for a profession which is being asked to develop a range of new skills to tackle the new objectives they have been asked to pursue.

On a more immediately practical plane, at school level, the possibility of accepting the broad responsibility towards pupils, envisaged in *Aspects of Secondary Education in England* (DES, 1979), begins with the headteacher. A head can easily check the level of his commitment to pastoral care by analysing his allocation of resources to non-academic pursuits; timetabling, recruitment of staff, distribution of enhanced salary posts and finance are areas where management skills can be used to solve the apparently intractable problems involved in accepting a whole school pastoral responsibility. Positive action too (the organising of workshops, seminars and further professional training) can add status and expertise to the pastoral activity of the school.

By using resources external to the school, further aids for children can be found. Colleges and departments of education, advisers, careers officers and social workers can all contribute effectively in helping to solve the problems of time and resources. The result of the acceptance of professional responsibility beyond the academic, and the exploration of possible resources in responding to that responsibility, will frequently lead to a reduction in the time-consuming and exhausting activity of containment of trouble – sitting on the cauldron lid with a nervy crisis team attacking periodic escapes by imposing further pressure.

How might we, then, recover some of the intimate knowledge of children that we used to have in our small schools and make inroads into the anonymity which characterises so many of our secondary schools?

Underlying the success of all school activity is the commitment of the teaching staff. That, of course, emphasises the tragic nature of the current anti-teacher sentiments so prevalent in some sections of the media. Should teachers be pushed into the more remote postures seen as normal in many continental education systems, the destruction of an admired and special British perspective in education would be complete, and one fears irreversible. The danger of the species 'magister novem ad quattour' – the nine-til-four teacher – has undoubtedly been increased by the contractual focus given to teachers' service. Understandable though the phenomenon is (at least everyone knows where they are), it is possible now that pupils learn from their contractual relationship with teachers that commitment is limited, and that the warmth and mutually respecting relationship that existed previously is less likely. Many parents have been the recipients – and teachers the generous donors – of the benefits of school plays, choirs, bands, sporting events, quiet chats and calm counsel. These are the types of contact that will ensure the regular finding of needles in haystacks. They are very hard to slot into a contractual relationship. From the teacher who does demonstrate a degree of commitment beyond the contractual, the pupils will continue to learn that they are valued, and will respond with the trust and confidence necessary in effective pastoral relationships. The more a school can offer teachers for whom the contract is a barely relevant necessity, the more likely will that school's pupils be to prosper. It must, however, be stated very strongly that the gross exploitation of goodwill, commitment and service (whether the professionals be nurses or teachers) will damage that service almost beyond repair. Pastoral care depends on governments as well as teachers and, given the Home Secretary's recently expressed concern that pupils should learn their civic duties in school (*Independent*, 12 July 1988), it should be of interest that the extensive survey carried out by Rutter *et al.* (1979) indicated that in schools where great attention was paid to the way pupils were dealt with as individuals, and to the ethos of the school as a social institution, much could be done to foster good behaviour and attainments, and that 'even in a disadvantaged area schools can be a force for good'!

We can learn, further, from colleagues in commerce and industry that low morale and limited commitment is energy sapping in itself. The evidence suggests that high degrees of staff commitment and increased morale reduce the need for enervating control strategies – and, more important, give a psychological lift to the personnel involved. Whatever direction we take, we arrive back at the same conclusion. Careful attention to, and scrutiny of, the social climate of the school will reduce tension and enhance the quality of everyone's life there (Cleugh, 1971; Everard, 1984, 1986).

The position strongly expressed in the earlier chapters of this book is that the most potent contribution, positively or negatively, to our pupils' personal development is the 'academic curriculum'. That position inevitably makes me strongly critical of both safety net views of pastoral care and supplementary (special pastoral curriculum) approaches. Teaching, though, must be realistic. We do need a safety net (though it should pick up only a sprinkling of difficult cases when we get the general curriculum more on target) and we do need the supplementation of PSE/tutorial periods while we continue our progress towards a realistic and more sophisticated curricular response to the pupils' personal development.

Whatever stage of development characterises a school's pastoral system, it needs data as a solid base for its decision-making. It is useful to remind ourselves that data is not an intrinsically valuable commodity. 'Unless you know what you need to decide, there is no point in giving a test; no measurement is useful by itself, but only when used in conjunction with other information.' (Milner, 1974) Amassing data in a purposeless way can overwhelm the decision-making process – or worse, given spurious legitimacy to doubtful conclusions.

Professor Black's (1988) report to the Secretary of State for Education is a model of judicious comment on the potential of testing as one aspect of the educational endeavour. The report is written by professionals who know that 'the system (of testing) should be so set up and operated as to have sensitive regard to its limited role, because the national curriculum and assessment are but part of the whole school curriculum.' (The Black Report, DES, 1988, p 30) Numbers are seductive; computers confer an apparent legitimacy on data – we have even developed a language which reflects the values we place on different kinds of data. There is a group of educators who ask for the 'hard' data of test results, as opposed to the 'soft' data of teacher assessment and observation. Can we not challenge the value-laden language? Is not quantification 'gross' where qualitative data is 'detailed', numbers 'brittle' where words are 'sensitive'?

It would be to over-simplify were I to leave such a dichotomous view of data assembly. The reality is that both quantitative and qualitative information will allow us closer access to our pupils' progress – two searchlights shining from different perspectives to minimise shadow. The anxiety is not primarily on the value of the various data collected but, to return to Milner, the purpose of the data collection. Will, for example, the information elicited from pupils at age 7, 11 and 14 be used *formatively*, ie in a pupil-centred way, to encourage and enhance motivation? On the other hand, will the data be used in a *summative* way, ie to permit others to make judgements about the pupils, in references to employers, institutes of further and higher education? Further, will the tests be used to make judgements about the school, comparing it with other schools in the area? Can both aims be pursued by the same tests? And what of *catalytic* data, ie information which permits the school to refine its own practice and development?

These central issues seem not to have been addressed, one suspects because the major intent is the elicitation of summative data, ie information on which judgements about pupils and schools will be made. If this is so, it is essential that Black's caveat be written boldly over all summative reports: 'Have sensitive regard to the limited role of testing', perhaps adding 'Insensitive use of testing is dangerous for the nation's educational health.' How would one quantify the patiently planned interaction between a teacher and an abused child that culminates, after a term's sensitive work, in the child's first-ever smile in school? It would be sad to think that such an achievement is no longer to be valued in the new dispensation.

There is another danger in insensitive testing with summative intent. Many teachers will remember (at least as former pupils) the stultifying effect of the old 11-plus examination – the grind of effort towards highly specific and limited attainments. Summative appraisal is the generator of defensive teaching in which schools and teachers will inevitably protect themselves by reducing innovatory risk-taking and creativity. The danger is that we will all play safe. It will be a foolish irony if the enterprise culture snuffs out creativity in school.

Part of the problem is that we have been here before. The dull ache of the 'payment by results' experiment of the latter part of the nineteenth century persists in the teaching profession like a hangover. Reactions to the establishment of an Assessment of Performance Unit were swift and negative, presumably as a result of this long-ingrained doubt that the results of teaching are accessible to meaningful testing. Teachers will say that the educative process is such a complex interaction, with so many variables involved as possible explanations of differential results, that test scores have little value. I recall the horror with which I learned that pupils about to begin my Spanish course had been previously given a 'language aptitude test'. What if Cindy Fabriccio, who scored so well on the test and had 'high language aptitude', should fail her exam after two years with me? My fears were based on the false assumption that only two variables in Cindy's language attainment existed – her aptitude and my teaching skill. We knew the former was high, so failure to attain would indicate that the latter was low.

Now we face the testing and appraisal requirements of the new Education Act. As with the testing movement of the late nineteenth century, the problem is not that we do not need educational data. It is our fear that information drawn for educational purposes will be used for political or ideological advantage. Again, as a profession, we must support the detailed cautions advised by the Black Report, ensuring that testing is genuinely pupil-centred.

Scepticism is an ideal base from which to analyse testing. Suspicions about over-simplification, doubts about excessive conclusions, and reservations that this test has anything useful to say about this situation, all help to remove a major element of danger in testing, ie that tests are in some way infallible or definitive. Savage (1968) offers an excellent summary of the potential and limitations of testing, and warns that 'the dangers of misinterpretation and catastrophe for the individual child ... must not be lightly brushed aside'. This anxiety is echoed ten years later by Rowntree (1977) who speaks of tests thus: 'The most well-intentioned acts often produce results other than those intended. We fail to comprehend the phenomenon being studied if we concern ourselves merely with a narrow range of ... publicly proclaimed effects and overlook its side effects'. The widespread reservations in the profession about testing at least ensure that there will be no light brushing aside.

However, that said, the opposite evil of educational decision-making based on hunch, on whim, on prejudice or intuition seems more attuned to witch-doctoring than a professional activity like teaching. Increasingly refined testing instruments are available to teachers and a total rejection of this important (and limited) source of information about our pupils puts the teacher in the position of the motorist who chooses to have a car with no instrumentation. He can drive, quite effectively, while his car is in good condition, but he has only the haziest idea of the running condition of this vehicle. Major problems, potential breakdown, greater capacity or excessive strain will only be detected by chance, as a result of enormous familiarity with one vehicle or when everything grinds to a halt. No driver relies exclusively on his instruments – they are not definitive – but it would be a foolish driver who pressed on regardless after an instrument had flashed a warning to him that all was not well.

So it is with testing in educational situations. We have available a wide range of 'instruments' which can give early indications of capacity, strain, problems and potential. It would be a foolish teacher who viewed test results as an infallible statement about an individual child's situation, but he would be no more foolish than the teacher who had received test results suggesting major problems, greater capacity or potential breakdown in a child and then ignored them.

Tests offer one piece of fallible information; they are descriptive not definitive. By careful selection from the wide range of available tests, we can gather information pertinent to the task of individualising the children in our schools – but tests are one piece in a complex jigsaw, not the final answer to a riddle. The question to be tackled is this: under the provision of the 1988 Education Reform Act, how can we as professionals ensure that the tests and appraisals we do will benefit the children rather than enhance someone's political career? Too many young lives were profoundly damaged by the 11-plus examination for us to stand irresponsibly by allowing it to happen again.

There is no doubt that the Black Report addresses the central educational issues and proposes sound responses compatible with educational endeavour – that the profession is committed to gauging the extent to which it succeeds in its learning objectives, that criterion-referenced tests do permit a more secure base on which to develop curricula, that the appraisal focus should be formative and child-focused. Yet one still feels a slight anxiety that the committee's statement that the principal purpose of schooling is 'children's learning' will be interpreted in a myriad different ways. Are we to assess their ability to become successful adults? If so, the evidence addressed earlier suggests that we must concentrate on socio-emotional outcomes as fundamental in achieving that aim. Are we to limit testing to the foundation subject of the national curriculum? If so, is there not a danger that parents, pupils and the community at large will value what is tested, because it is tested, rather than what is important? The caring, practical implementation of the Black Report will tell us whether, to use his report's phrase, 'assessment is to be the servant not the master'.

As long as the profession insists that we collect data which focuses consistently on pupil need, the appraisal requirements of the new Act will emerge with the positive effects Black and his colleagues intend. If ever appraisal in school is used as a tool of financial management or political decision-making, Black's recommendations will be shown to have been dreadfully naïve.

Teachers, of course, collect information in many subtle and sensitive ways, more deeply and precisely than any test could. Appraisal of social and emotional progress offers data on how children are progressing in these fundamental areas, and the manner of collecting that data varies from the most informal observations in school playgrounds to more structured attempts to answer the complex question, 'who are our pupils?'

The social and emotional development of children, as indicated earlier, has important consequences in school performance. Thus data on socio-emotional development must be readily available for teachers. One of the most widely used instruments in this area is the Bristol Social Adjustment Guide (BSAG). Three separate analyses look at the child in residential care, in the family and in school – the latter is clearly the one most useful to the teacher. The manual claims that the BSAG offers 'a quick means by which ... guidance counsellors can keep themselves informed of children's adjustment and get insights into reasons for learning disability'. It goes on to explain that teachers can be taught to recognise maladjustment and that the guide will help them to adopt 'an objective professional attitude' to what is commonly regarded as 'bad' behaviour. This instrument is easy to use in that it calls on the teacher simply to underline those of a series of descriptions of child behaviour which describe the subject's behaviour under such general headings as 'Attitudes to teacher', 'Attitudes to school work' or 'Personal ways'. When the specific behaviours are underlined, a transparent template is placed over each page of the guide, and underlined items which match the template markings are recorded on a diagnostic form, which clearly analyses the degree and nature of any maladjustment.

A more recently developed instrument, the Lewis Counselling Inventory (NFER, 1980), is designed to provide teachers with a convenient instrument for identifying pupils who may benefit from a sensitive offer of counselling. It can help to highlight areas of particular concern, and is seen by its authors as an aid to teachers in increasing their understanding of their classes. The inventory examines six areas:

1. Relationships with teachers.
2. Relationships with family.
3. Irritability.
4. Social confidence.
5. Relationships with peers.
6.. Health.

The pupil's agreement or disagreement with short statements on each topic and his replies form the basis of the assessment.

There is no easily used measure of self-esteem, though the existence of this quality in children is crucial to their healthy psychological development. A questionnaire devised by D H Hamblin (1974) does, however, help to give teachers/counsellors and their pupils a degree of insight into this aspect of emotional development. Hamblin uses the hypothesis that self-esteem is achieved when there is a high degree of harmony or congruence between our 'self-image' (the perception we have of ourself) and our 'ideal self' (the ideal at which we would like to arrive) (cf Chapter 2). Burns (1979; 1982) offers further insight into this crucial area of pupil development.

His quesionnaire asks children to agree that a list of statements is 'like me' or 'not like me', and thus arrives, by exploring attitudes to school, peers, the future, family, and so on, at a fairly accurate 'self-image' of each pupil. Some days later the same list of statements is presented to the child, who this time is asked to tick according to whether he 'would like to be like that' or 'would not like to be like that'. By comparing the first set of answers with the second the pupil and his teacher can see how far he 'is' what he 'would like to be'.

Clearly this is not the standardised, statistically analysed kind of test we have looked at previously, but it provides more information in that vital task of individualising children. The Hamblin questionnaire is, in any case, an excellent base for a discussion in the tutorial period, and can give the teacher further insights into the group.

The success with which pupils are able to interact with peers is, as Kohlberg's, Nicholson's and Heath's research points out, an important predictive indicator of later success as an adult. An interesting and useful means of appraising the interactive characteristics of a group of pupils is the sociogram. It is used to expose to the teacher the patterns of interaction within a group of children such as cliques, pairs, isolates and cleavages which can all be revealed by this instrument. Clearly, the personal interrelationships of pupils do have classroom consequences, and knowledge of the group's dynamics will help teachers to plan seating, group work, and co-operative activities to better effect. In addition, the withdrawn child, who rarely causes any disruption, is identified and assistance can be offered quickly. The sociogram is a simple and flexible instrument to use. Several approaches are possible, but a simple and productive approach is to ask the children three questions:

Who would you like to sit with?
Who would you like to do class work with?
Who would you like to go on holiday with?

They are asked to make their choice from the members of their own class. It is important that the process is one of choosing not rejecting, and that no child should have feelings of isolation intensified. When all the choices are made, they are marked against a list of the children's names. To simplify the explanation, we can look at an example of a small group of eight pupils (Figure 4.2).

From this information the teacher can construct a 'target' sociogram (Figure 4.3) which will present its information in an easily comprehensible, visual form. The number in each circle indicates the number of choices received by pupils in that circle; thus rapid identification of the isolate, Tom, is possible. Also the boy/girl friendship groups, the pairing and reciprocation of friendship can be seen at a glance and analysed.

The girls' subgroups are more open, less intense than the tight cohesiveness of the boys' triangular friendship with excludes Tom. In a large class it may be worth while simplifying the process by giving

	Dan	Joe	Tom	Fred	Mary	Barbara	Avril	Sue
Dan		111						
Joe	11			1				
Tom		11		1				
Fred	1	11						
Mary						1	11	
Barbara					1		11	
Avril						1		11
Sue					1	1	1	
Total choices received by each pupil	3	7	0	2	2	3	5	2

Each pupil has three choices which are entered horizontally on the chart, under the name of the chosen child.

Figure 4.2 *A sociogram choice chart*

only one or two choices to the children. The principle is simple. By using it thoughtfully teachers will find insights into the structure of their groups which will help in the individualisation of constituent members, using friendships and group cohesiveness in positive ways and making early intervention to help isolates.

The large secondary school makes it difficult to establish the kinds of personal contacts with pupils that have characterised smaller schools. One way to accumulate a more comprehensive and perceptive picture of pupils is to establish case conferences as a feature of the 'pupil individualisation' programme. Most teachers have experienced the informal 'case conference' which occurs in a staffroom, when a pupil's name arises accidentally as a result of his behaviour in lessons. Frequently, several useful insights and related experiences observed by teachers immediately emerge and help to shed light on the possible explanation, response to and outcome of the problem. The only drawback with this *ad hoc* approach is that it is accidental. In large institutions if we want things to happpen we need to plan for them to happen and to check afterwards to see that they have happened.

Formalising the case conference would not be intended to replace informal professional conversations but to supplement them and underpin them. I was greatly helped in relating to my pupils by the

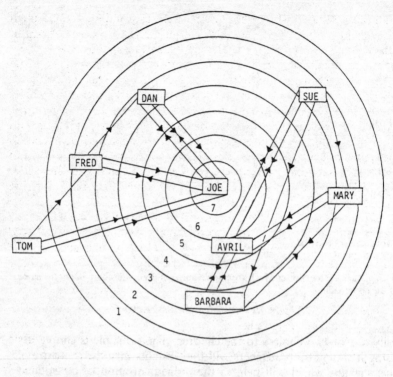

Arrows indicate direction of choice
Reciprocated choice is indicated thus: ➤◄

Figure 4.3 *A target sociogram*

practice I experienced in one secondary school of publishing a list of names weekly, about whom there would be a case conference. Any teacher could put a name on the list if he felt he was short on information about a pupil, and any teacher who was able to supply information pertinent to the school's task was expected to attend the conference and speak. The list varied in length, and as the year went on the children with chronic difficulties became better known to the staff. Our experience was that the fuller information made our teaching and social response more appropriate. Children who found themselves having to cope with some acute problems (bereavement, parental separation, imprisonment of a parent) were identified more quickly and the relevant information communicated to a wider group of staff.

Thus, if I noticed 'Mary Thompson' on the list for discussion, though I had no problem with her, I would go along to the conference to enlarge my perception of her life, her background, and so on.

In complex and severe cases it is professionally desirable to invite other professionals involved in the case to a case conference; social workers, education welfare officers, youth workers can frequently bring important new insights to the difficulties a school faces with a pupil. We will examine in greater detail the importance of liaison with 'outside agencies' in later chapters. The professional demarcation disputes which have long marred relationships between the social and education services can be no source of pride for either side. They have helped no one, and may well have harmed some of our most deprived children.

There is an extensive literature drawing our attention to the family as an important (and occasionally problematic) data source. Craft *et al* (1970) and his colleagues assembled a range of evidence on the influence home had on school performance, and McBeath, Mearns and Smith (1986) have extended, modernised and deepened our understanding of that relationship. They uncompromisingly direct our attention to a factor in education which is theoretically recognised as crucial, but practically almost ignored, ie the influence of the home. The evidence that parents constitute the single most important variable in a pupil's performance is incontrovertible, yet frequently parents feel pushed out, snubbed and ignored. Ideally parents should be involved in the education of their children right through their school life, and teachers need to develop the skill of using parental interest and eagerness to help (cf Chapter 5).

Of course, many children have parents who have entirely negative attitudes to school, and an appropriate school response here would be to support the child and supplement as far as possible the deficiencies in parental interest and encouragement. Home visiting by school staff is fraught with difficulties but is not impossible. Durham County was among the first to attach social workers directly to schools, and many headteachers have deliberately encouraged a critical but constructive Parent Teachers Association to offer the layman's view of the professional's performance. As with all the means outlined for gaining greater contact with and insight into our pupils, contact with parents can be seen as an important principle to be implemented, according to the creative skills of the staff and the opportunities offered in specific situations. The vast majority of parents recognise the professional expertise of teachers. The odd know-all ought not to be allowed to break the most influential alliance on behalf of children – between their teachers and their parents.

Finally, we must not forget that most schools do use supplementary pastoral input via tutorial or PSE periods. If a child suffers from vitamin deficiency, we do not decide that only a proper diet will suffice – we give vitamin supplements. So it is with a curriculum not yet fully sensitive to its pastoral potential – the tutorial period can be used to supplement its inadequacies.

When a large number of staff are willing to involve themselves energetically in the pastoral system (for this to occur both the leadership and management skills of the headteacher are vital) time can be productively allocated to 'pastoral activities' during the school day. Although some comprehensive schools do offer such timetable slots and use a carefully constructed syllabus, many of the teachers questioned by Best *et al.* (1977) saw the timetabled guidance slot as an opportunity to 'facilitate petty administrative functions', and others find that their school makes no provision in the timetable for this part of the children's education.

As with any other use of school time, pastoral periods must be examined initially in terms of the goals they pursue. How do we expect the children to have changed as a result of two three-quarters of an hour periods devoted to PSE? What will they subsequently be able to do that they cannot do now? What new attitudes will they be able to explore? In other words, we must set out our objectives clearly. These will, of course, vary according to the age, background, and current developmental level of the children, but again two clear focuses seem to be needed:

1. To offer situations to the children in which as wide a range as possible of the skills appropriate to them as individuals can be developed. Specifically they are the skills outlined below.
2. To individualise the children in the group so that developmental retardation, stress and social inadequacy can be identified, and sympathetic remedial responses initiated.

Several authors have identified areas which might be tackled in the tutorial period. Thus we find a pioneer in Mahler (1969, pp 24–9) who suggests as areas particularly accessible to the process of group counselling:

1. The ability to understand better a variety of people and to see how others perceive things.
2. The ability to respect the views of others, yet not feel that one's

own perception of reality is without value.
3. The development of social competence.
4. Learning to share with other people, experiencing a sense of participation.

Although he was not talking specifically about the tutorial period, one might add Hamblin's areas of concern (1974, pp 172–87) as also accessible to group techniques. He argues that the following skills are vital in establishing a mature outlook on life:

1. Decision-making skill.
2. Standpoint-taking ability.
3. The ability to delay gratification.

Finally, some of the items from Hopson and Hough's (1976, p 18) model of personal growth can be developed using group techniques.

1. The ability to accept and deal with negative feelings.
2. The ability to offer and receive help.
3. The ability to initiate and maintain relationships.
4. The ability to be assertive effectively.
5. The ability to create and manage problem-solving.

Role-play, simulation, problem-solving, exercises, structured discussion and value-clarification exercises are some of the techniques available to pursue these aims, and a wide range of commercially available material is being used by teachers (Hopson and Scally, 1986; Brandes and Phillips, 1979; Kirk, 1987).

Having emphasised the need to systematise data-gathering in a large school, I would not want to leave the impression that *informal data-gathering* was without value. Contact with pupils in sport and drama often gives teachers opportunities to see hidden talents and possibilities for success in unlikely places; they may, conversely, be the first situations in which problems show. The intimacy of school trips and holidays permit mutual respect bonds to be established that years of grind at irregular verbs or English grammar would never yield. The skilled observer in the playground, dining hall and corridors will spot not only the heartbroken isolate sobbing behind the biology labs, but also those tiny nuances in child behaviour that serve as early warnings of trouble.

This chapter has been about individualising pupils as a prerequisite to responding appropriately to their needs. Significantly, we needed to start by examining staff attitudes and find ourselves concluding by looking at staff expertise in the skills of observation. It is a clear reminder that teachers must be at the heart of pastoral activity. The instruments are no more than tools, however useful. It is the teaching profession which must translate accumulated information into educational response. Nevertheless, educational response must be based on sound data, not impressions, if problems are to be tackled. We do have the means of collecting such data and owe it to children to 'know' them as well as we possibly can. Figure 4.1, page 62, outlines an overview of the responsibilities we have in this area.

Chapter 5

Needles in Haystacks

Our methods of assembling data on individuals have become increasingly sophisticated during the 1980s. Large companies subject prospective employees to tests, to detailed problem-solving exercises, to experiential, simulated tests of decision-making, even to the analysis of their handwriting. The previous chapter suggests that schools will be expected to follow in accumulating masses of information on their charges – garnered in both informal and formal methods of appraisal. The problem is not how to collect such information, it is rather how to make sure that such mountains of detail as we can gather are set at the service of pupils above all – again, Black's plea that appraisal should be a servant not a master. There is very little disagreement with the view that we should keep records; where parents, teachers, politicians and employers divide is on the issues:

What are the records for?
What information should they contain?
Who should contribute to them?
Who should have access to them?
Should the law be involved in the issue?

In so far as there is an *official* position, it is vague and rhetorical. Plowden (1967) recommended that 'a detailed folder on each child' should be kept. It was suggested that the folder be used as a 'basis' for a regular review of the child with his parents. In some schools the interpretation of Plowden's suggestion is that the class or headteacher will *select* what he regards as pertinent material from the records, thus offering a censored version as the review basis and, in effect, limiting parental access to the record. In other, fewer, schools, the record is a tabled document for such a review, and both parents and school staff have equal access to it.

More recently the DES consultative document *Education in Schools* (1977) appears to take a much firmer line, suggesting:

> The need for keeping school records of the educational development of individual children has long been recognised. It is more than ever true today that clear and reliable records of progress are necessary if individual help and counselling are to be provided.

The document, however, lapses into the familiar but insubstantial exhortation that 'high standards of professional accuracy' and '*reasonable* consistency or practice' should be pursued. We get little help as teachers with unravelling the concept 'high standards of professional accuracy', and finish up as a profession with wild variations in practice over the country.

Perhaps a crisper and more helpful approach appeared in the Warnock Report (1978). The report deals with the child who has special educational needs, but its suggestions on records have a clarity which is absent in earlier statements, and which can be generalised to include all pupils:

> Records of an individual child's performance should be clear, factual, up-to-date and reliable ... and readily available for consultation. Parents should as a matter of course be able to see their child's folder. (pp 54 and 419)

Although the Warnock Committee was quite clear in its recommendations, it must be borne in mind that, to date, there has been no official acceptance of its proposal. It was, however, a straw in the wind. Public opinion is now moving towards much greater accountability in the compilation of school records and, as part of that accountability, a recognition of parental right of access to them.

A Commons question from Max Madden to the Under-Secretary of State for Education and Science (*Hansard* 954, 229–38, 1978) gave early voice to a growing view. In his question, he described the parental right of access to school records on their children as a 'basic freedom', which ought to be recognised by statute. Madden argued cogently that, since the school record card had such an important influence on the child's progress in school, in higher education, and in his initial attempts to enter the world of work, it should be subject to strict scrutiny. His enquiries revealed that gross distortions, factual inaccuracies and opinions, masquerading as objective judgement, had found their way on to children's cards. There was no suggestion that this was commonplace, but there was a strong plea that to avoid even occasional lapses of that kind the prevailing tight secrecy surrounding children's records should be relaxed.

American schools have been using a more open approach to records for 14 years. From 1974, parents were given right of access to the records kept on their children, and a right to an explanation of items contained in them. This type of approach would have prevented, or made less likely, the grosser errors discovered by Madden. He cites that a child in nursery school was described on a record card as 'unreliable and a source of difficulty'. In this case, the parents, under the American system, would have been able to question the entry; in what sense is a pre-five-year-old described as 'unreliable'? What behaviour led to the description that the child was 'a source of difficulty'? At the least, parental access to this type of entry would make us, as teachers, distinguish clearly between factual statements and personal opinions.

In another example, Madden describes how a boy, accused of taking money with menaces, and later found not guilty, discovered that his 'crime' had remained on his school record card. Here, too, parental access might have prevented a serious error. Similarly, a statement by a teacher that she is 'a bit concerned over S's honesty – though as yet have no evidence' is a gratuitous slur on a child, which would not happen if, as teachers, we knew parents could see record card entries. Simply following the Warnock recommendation to be 'factual and reliable' would make our entries a firmer base for judging a child.

It is to be expected that on some occasions teacher and parent will disagree with each other in their assessment of a child; in such cases, the American system gives right of appeal to parents. If the original statement is eventually deemed proper, the parent is permitted to add his own dissenting note to the record, on the quite proper assumption that a child may well present entirely different behaviour at home and at school. In addition to this intense parental involvement in record-keeping, the American law now also requires that all requests for access to the record be noted, and that parents be reminded of all their rights on an annual basis.

Since, in this country, we do not yet have a teachers' council which might have been charged with the task of producing a coherent policy on records, it seems probable that central or local government will take decisions that teachers ought to take themselves. That should not prevent individual schools from subjecting this important part of the educational endeavour to the closest scrutiny. We have no official or specific legal requirements on the form, content and level of confidentiality of school record cards but, by looking at the purpose of the cards, our attitudes towards privacy and the protection of parental and child rights, it is possible to produce a fully professional and effective record system.

In an extension of the Record of Personal Achievement Scheme mentioned in Chapter 1, we have seen a considerable expansion of the approach to record-keeping described as *profiling*. This approach differs considerably from earlier methods which tried to encapsulate a pupil's character on a piece of card. The criticisms of Madden were directed at such earlier attempts to present a school view of a pupil to an outside organisation. Their intent was essentially summative and judgemental, their scope usually limited to academic performance and discipline, their content teacher-controlled, access to them severely restricted and their effect on the relationships of all involved in producing them constraining.

The extensive movement towards profiling intends to alter that thrust, increasing and giving priority to the formative, motivating potential of recording, including the full range of pupil talent and interests within the content, encouraging pupil participation in their formulation and making them the kind of open communication that fosters trusting relationships. In my view the best survey of this topic is still the seminal review by Law (1984), though the range of excellently produced books on this topic increases each year (Balogh, 1982; Garforth and MacKintosh, 1986; DES, 1977a, 1984, 1985, 1988).

Everyone engaged in the process of education – pupils, parents, teachers, administrators, employers, politicians – needs secure databases on which to form their decisions. Each of us is making different kinds of decisions, despite some considerable overlap. Given the present variety of decision-making focus, the generation of a comprehensive and suitable database is enormously complex. The needs of all those interested parties need, somehow, to be met. Cartwright and Cartwright (1974) argue this:

> Doctors and lawyers seek data. Lawyers know that hunches won't stand up in court ... Similarly a doctor knows he can't indiscriminately prescribe ... he needs diagnostic data. Although seldom in situations as glamorous as those of the 'detective' lawyer and the 'detective' doctor, teachers are detectives too. (They) should assemble as much factual information as possible before taking instructional decisions.

In 1974 they spoke of 'instructional decisions'; we have learned that such detailed data is needed for all our decisions in school – educational rather than instructional. Seen in this context, the record card takes on a new significance. As is the case in the legal and medical professions, all involved in education must accept that impression, unsubstantiated opinion, factual error and out-of-date material have no place in the decision-making process.

The existence of the record card is a practical response to a number of phenomena characteristic of our society. Our schools are no longer the homely group of 300 pupils they once were. Increased numbers mean that we cannot hold in our heads pertinent data on all our pupils as we once could. In addition to the increase in the size of our schools, both our pupil population and our staff are more mobile than previously; children arrive for a two-year stay and move on; a successful year head becomes a deputy head in a school 200 miles away. In this situation, informal information storage provides no means of ensuring stability and continuity in our basis for decision-making. With a record card, properly used, teachers and pupils can move schools, leaving the educational decision-making base firm for all concerned.

The argument seems to be incontrovertible, yet when I recently came across a difficult adolescent girl in a large comprehensive school, I asked the head if I could see the girl's record card. I was astonished to see that the card contained only her name, address, date of birth and the 'information' that her average mark in ten subjects had been 53.7. The card contained spaces for comment on general health, parents' views on the pupil's future, noteworthy activities and interests, test scores, teachers' estimates of personality, attendance record and general comments. This difficult jigsaw, Janice, had to be tackled with three-quarters of the pieces missing.

Many teachers, fortunate enough to work with a more effective record system than that described above, will tend to dismiss the example as exceptional. However, the HMI report, *Aspects of Secondary Education* (1979), did find that over one-third of the record systems examined for the report were inadequate (Chapter 9, para 3.14).

There has been considerable increased awareness of the importance of records since then, but perhaps it is now appropriate to list the purposes of a record card, and then to use that analysis as a basis for constructing (a) a record card, and (b) a records system. The cumulative record system should facilitate the following school activities:

1. The ability to respond to each child as an *individual* across the full range of his talents.

2. The ability to engage in sound *curriculum planning*, based on comprehensive knowledge of all the pupils.
3. The ability to provide, when it is sought, sensitive *counselling*.
4. The ability to offer sound educational and career *guidance*, designed to enhance and maximise the talents of each child.
5. The establishment of productive *liaison* with the pupil's *family* and, where necessary, *outside agencies*.
6. The ability to offer to prospective *employers* and institutes of extended education *negotiated and agreed information*, pertinent to the next stage in the pupil's life.

Children very rarely arrive at secondary school without an induction programme being provided. Part of that programme normally includes the passing on of records from the feeder primary school. Ideally this record should have been discussed with the parents and, in an appropriate way, the child who is making the transfer. Records from the child's previous school will normally form the basis of the new record card. This information may need to be re-cast to fit the format of the secondary school's card. All information received ought to be factual/behavioural, not opinion. A statement that 'this child is the most aggressive child I have met in ten years' teaching' is useless, and should not be transferred to a new record card. It may tell us more about the school or the teacher than the child. Since one teacher can describe as 'boisterous and lively' behaviour what another teacher would describe as 'uncontrolled and insolent', we need to know the behaviour and the behaviour should be recorded in an unadorned way. Compare

> George was playing football in the school yard. Harry came over, picked up the ball and walked off with it. George hit Harry and said, 'Give us it, you bugger.' Harry dropped the ball and walked away.

and

> George was contentedly playing football in the school yard. Harry bowled cheerfully along and picked up the ball, running off with it. George bashed Harry and screamed, 'Give us it, you bugger.' Harry reluctantly dropped the ball and walked away (adapted from Cartwright and Cartwright [1974]).

The first version is factual; the teacher who wrote it presents us with facts, not his interpretation of the facts. The second version contains several non-factual, interpretive items; 'contentedly', 'bowled cheerfully along', 'bashed', 'screamed' and 'reluctantly' may be accurate but they are expressions of opinion. Of course, the teacher's immediate response to a child in a classroom or school yard is based on his reading of a whole range of behavioural, verbal and non-verbal signals. Our reaction, here and now, to a child, is based on our opinion about whether he is exhibiting dry humour, insolence, aggression, forcefulness, determination, seriousness, caution or lack of initiative; the important distinction is between our 'now' interaction with pupils and the crystallisation of a fallible teacher perception into a permanent record. If we record observed behaviour, we allow subsequent readers to form their own opinion; if we record our opinion, then we block the subsequent readers' access to the original behaviour. Warnock's recommendation that records should be factual is fundamental, and my view is that each entry should, in addition, be dated and signed by the teacher who entered it.

So far, in constructing our record card, we would have a folder which contains information from the child's primary school and the outside of the folder itself which will contain basic biographical information (Figure 5.1).

What will be useful to us as secondary school-teachers? One important message to the new pupil is that his view is important. In the final weeks of third term in the junior school, as part of the induction programme, each transferring pupil can be asked: 'What would you like your new teachers to know about you? Share with them some of the interesting things you've done at this school.' With a little help the pupils will soon become eager contributors to their own record folder, and receiving teachers will be introduced to the new pupils' way of looking at the school world. In addition to providing an initial, if simple, contribution to their record card, they will begin to tackle that key, life-long question 'who am I?' in a structured way.

Of course, the school itself will send forward information – ideally, discussed with parents at the final parent–teacher meeting of the third term. The reality is that the quality of information sent forward by the primary school varies enormously (indeed, some primary schols send on excellent data which is wasted by the secondary school) but the 'primary school sheet', in the secondary school folder, is an important data baseline. The precise format is relatively unimportant, but the receiving secondary school should have precise information on the pupil's reading ability, performance in number activities, verbal ability (much learning is done in discussion), his socio-emotional skills with family, peers and other adults, and his interests and aptitudes. The receiving teacher would select the major items for this résumé. It is perhaps worth bearing in mind that the NFER and Hillingdon LEA

```
TOLLEY, TONY
D.O.B.  24/1/74

10, SALISBURY COURT, DEELAND, BRADLEIGH, HANTS.  TEL: 63827

EMERGENCY CONTACT     FATHER (ANTHONY TOLLEY)
                      WELTON ENGINEERING, SOUTHAMPTON STREET,
                      PORTSMOUTH, TEL: 82748

                      MOTHER (MARY TOLLEY)
                      (9 - 12 noon) WOOLWORTH'S, HIGH STREET,
                      PORTSMOUTH.  TEL: 83333.

SIBLINGS: MARY  - 16 yrs.
          ROBERT - 14 yrs.
```

Figure 5.1. *Record card container*

have produced a 'Transitional Assessment Module' which is designed specifically to perform the task of facilitating transfer from junior to secondary school.

While the appraisal requirements of the national curriculum are still being formulated, schools will have to rely on other methods to give a clear picture to the receiving secondary school of the pupil's general status at the time of entry into the new school. It remains important that a record is made of *behaviour*. An example of such a data sheet is given in Figure 5.2.

When factual information from the pupil's primary school has been assembled and summarised, an organised recognition of the importance of family involvement in education could well lead to a formal

---

Dear Mr and Mrs Tolley

We use school record cards in much the same way as your doctor uses his medical record cards, in order to help us meet our pupils' needs quickly and effectively. We would be grateful if you could send us any information that you think may help us to help your child get more out of school, any special health problems, particular interests or hobbies, difficulties at home, how he gets on with his brothers or sisters - anything you think will help us get to know your child better. Of course, all information will be restricted to those people who are responsible for the education of your child. Please feel free to come and see me if you have any queries or worries. Your child's record card will be open to you as we feel that educating him is a team effort, involving school and family.

I enclose a reply sheet and envelope for your convenience.

Yours sincerely

J FORSTER
Head of First Year

DATA ENTERED FROM PRIMARY SCHOOL RECORD BY: J. FORSTER SEPT. 6, 1984

PUPIL: A. Tolley   FEEDER: Bradleigh County Junior School. Tel: Bradleigh 4871

	Reading	Number	Verbal fluency	GENERAL COMMENT
A C A D E M I C	1.4.84.: Can tackle Janet & John (4), Beacon Readers (4) 5.6.79. Neale Test (Pupil 11 yrs, 5 months) Reading age 10.4	4.4.84.: Can tackle $+ - \times \div$ T.U. $\frac{1}{2} \frac{1}{4} \frac{1}{3} \frac{1}{8}$ Decimals. Linear Metric Measures, Square Metres, Time, Calendar, Weight — Metric	Rarely volunteers a remark cf. reading age. Vocabulary limited Local accent strong	Reading a little weak, but no major problem. Needs to develop self-confidence in speaking
	Family	*School adults*	*Peers*	
S O C I O - E M O T I O N A L	10.2.82. Grandfather died. Tony downcast for a month. Speaks regularly of parents (plays with father). Admires older brother	Asks to do jobs in school (milk, storing books, etc)—relates by doing, not talking	Never alone—star of Junior football team, swimmer. Spent time teaching his friend Neil to swim	Supportive family, secure child, possibly still affected by loss of grandfather
	Intellectual	*Sport/outdoor*	*Mechanical/manual*	
I N T E R E S T S	Feb./March 1983—Did excellent project on birds. Researched, written up, and illustrated	Soccer fanatic. Able swimmer—500 metres award; Bronze life saving	None known	

ATTENDANCE/HEALTH — No illness of note, only occasional one or two-day absences in past six years.

G. S. Winter.   See over for further information

Figure 5.2. *Secondary school record folder: sheet one, excerpt from primary school record*

invitation to parents to contribute to the record card. Schools at the moment will make their own decisions about the degree of parental access but, as we have seen earlier, the movement is towards extending parental access to records. To use this movement constructively, rather than to obstruct it, the school could include in a letter to parents of first-year pupils an explanation of the purpose of record cards, their right of access and how they would be able to help construct their child's card (see example on p 87). Of course, the response will vary enormously from family to family, but it invariably produces useful information – that the child is bilingual, that one sibling is adopted, that the father is unemployed, that the child cooks for the whole family and helps to care for an invalid mother. Since this quite intimate information comes voluntarily from the parents, a dated entry into the record card is entirely ethical. This liaison with the family ought to continue throughout the child's time at school. It will have particular significance when third-year option choices and career decisions are being made.

Two contrary problems present themselves when schools use this approach: the over-garrulous and the excessively taciturn or non-responder. The family who sends in reams of irrelevant data about the child liking gold top milk or beefburgers is not really difficult to handle – the teacher simply needs to select carefully. However, when no reply, a rude reply or an unhelpful reply arrives on the year head's desk, things are more difficult. Obviously, no compulsion or pressure can be exerted, so the exercise seems to be an abortive one. It can be argued, on the other hand, that it is useful to have the information that parents are not inclined to co-operate with the school, and the *fact* of the unco-operative reply should be recorded. The process of individualising the child is then well under way; the two major influences on the child's life so far, family and primary school, have made an input to our decision-making database, and the pupil too has learned that his contribution matters.

The fact that the school, the parent and the pupil will have to make decisions which will affect the socio-emotional, academic and vocational development of the pupil means that data is needed in all these areas in order to carry out the task professionally. Thus a third group of record sheets is required, designed to store items on the socio-emotional, academic and vocational progress of the child. The data collected, again, will be factual, dated and signed, so that subsequent readers will be able to interpret effectively.

Socio-emotional progress

This section will record behavioural statements about the pupil's manner of relating to himself, to peers, teachers and, as far as is known, family. Self-esteem inventories can be used for group discussion in the tutorial period or in a one-to-one interview with a pupil; but more than that, they constitute evidence of progress, or lack of it, in the socio-emotional sphere. Similarly, a sociogram can be recorded if it shows an unusual social quality in a child. Children who (prima facie) present a major problem can be tested via the British Social Adjustment Guide. Dated recordings of results are important if they are to be useful. It is not only these formal procedures that are helpful to the teacher; opportunity should also be given for the recording of 'anecdotal' information, ie data on incidents which have been witnessed by the recorder, who then records these factually. These would include visits from parents, positive social interactions like working on school plays, and negative incidents like proved vandalism, bullying or truancy.

The suggested format of the record slips (Figures 5.3 and 5.4, pp 92 and 93) has tried to steer clear of rigidity, thereby directing the teacher's attention to specific items. Teachers are highly skilled in identifying significant behaviours, and this 'open' style of report gives scope for them to use that skill effectively. The size of entry will vary enormously; some children will have volumes written about them, others relatively little. The criteria for judging the quality of the record entries is whether or not they help the teaching staff to 'know' the child concerned.

Vocational/interest progress

Detecting the individual pupil's interests, right from his first year, helps to establish an excellent foundation for the social interaction teachers need with children. I recall a somewhat extreme case of an awkward 'punk' girl with spiky hair, 'decadent' make-up and outlandish clothes. She was quite intelligent but a disruptive influence in her class. My first contact with her involved a chat about punk 'culture', how long it took to apply the (to me) ghoulish eye make-up and black nail polish. That was our point of contact; German verbs then followed quite effectively after that contact had been established.

When schools operate the scheme, the Record of Personal Achievement can provide a rich source of information about pupils' interests. Later on careers interviews, vocational interest inventories and work experience should be entered along with the pupil's expressed aspirations.

Academic development

This part of the record should include information on the type of teaching situation (streamed, set, mixed ability, remedial group and major tendencies in performance). The school report cards sent out to parents should be duplicated and filed in the record to supply specific details on academic performance.

In addition to in-school assessments of performance, any objective tests of intelligence or attainment and (for the near future) results of the national testing programme should be entered, along with the date of the test, any recommendations for action and the results of action taken. As in the other areas on which information is required, we would expect to find variations in quantity of entry from child to child and year to year. In so far as we are seeking to individualise our pupils, a sparse record folder should be carefully scrutinised to ensure that it does not represent an anonymous child in our school. Of course, some children have a smooth, successful passage through school, and our records may reflect that by being smaller in quantity, but a careful check that academic competence is not distracting us from other pupil needs is important if we are to individualise our charges fully. Academic competence does not correlate with socio-emotional competence, any more than the reverse.

The collaborative construction of profiles is, of course, a powerful weapon in combating records of narrow perspective and limited view. Each informational emphasis identified earlier, and the various sources of such information (parents, primary schools, secondary school-teachers etc), will emphasise that the pupil's scrutiny of such information, though initially apparently threatening to adult status and professional autonomy, is a trend that can improve the quality of the records. The reciprocal influence of child response to our views of them, and our response to their view of themselves, can contribute powerfully to a supportive and enhancing reduction of adolescent egocentricity, and an increase in the care which we devote to the records we write.

The final major source of data on children is that range of social agencies with which many of us come into contact during our lives – the medical services, the social services, the police, the probation services etc. The learning potential of any pupil is altered by intervention from these agencies and it is entirely appropriate that information from them should be included in our decision-making information base. There is, of course, an implicit assumption here that there is effective liaison between the school and the outside agencies. Data from these sources

Sheet No, 1

PUPIL: A. TOLLEY   SOCIO-EMOTIONAL DEVELOPMENT

Year 1
1985–6   18.11.85   Hamblin Self-Esteem Inventory done in tutorial period—reveals large gap between self-concept and ideal self (−17). J.W.T. (Form Tutor)

24.11.85   (Theme of tutorial activity currently 'my group'.) Sociogram in class indicates he is on periphery of his group—has two close friends. cf. Primary School record—what has gone wrong? J.W.T.

18.1.86   Two admitted instances of truancy.
1.2.86

8.2.86   Parents visit school—very concerned, express eagerness to help and puzzlement. F.R.W.

15.2.86   Tony subject of case conference—several of his teachers say his work is of poor quality and that he participates little. Decision to try to use his sporting and artistic skills to raise self-esteem. J.W.T.

30.5.86   Hamblin Self-Esteem Inventory suggests things improving (−3). Tony regularly attends swimming club and is working on school play scenery. J.W.T.

Year 2
1986–7   8.9.86   Tony tells me in school yard that he 'couldn't wait to get back'. F.P.

10.10.86   Tony involved in brawl—investigation suggests it was a fight over the relative merits of football teams—one desk broken. Culprits to contribute to cost of repair. Parents contacted. F.P.

20.12.86   End of term play—Tony very involved on scenery construction (worked every night for two weeks 5–6.30 p.m.). F.P.

Figure 5.3. *Secondary school record: samples of entries (socio-emotional development)*

Sheet No. 1

VOCATIONAL/INTEREST DEVELOPMENT

PUPIL: A. TOLLEY

Year 1
1985–6   12.6.85   Tony has done paper round all this year.
6 a.m. rise—$1\frac{1}{2}$ hours work. J.W.T.

Year 2
1986–7   8.11.85   Tony has won local radio painting
competition—his entry 'Seagulls at Seal Sands'
won the under-14 class. He is showing great
talent in this area. F.P.

          4.5.86   Tony one of a group of eight, with Jeff
Thwaites (Art Teacher) supervising, painting
murals at local Playgroup—after school. F.P.

Sheet No. 1

PUPIL: A. TOLLEY   ACADEMIC DEVELOPMENT

(End of year reports are filed with this Document)

Year 1
1985–6   Class 1H   (full ability range—remedials withdrawn for
English and Maths.)

        12.7.85   Apart from Art, Nuffield Science and Tech.
Drawing, Tony is in bottom three in all
subjects (see attached report to parents for
details). J.W.T.

Year 2
1986–7   Class 2H   (set for Maths and French)

        14.7.86   Tony remains poor in academic subjects. No
lack of effort.

Figure 5.4. *Secondary school record: sample entries*
(vocational/interest and academic)

93

should be entered either as documents/reports/letters submitted by them or approved summaries of conversations, written by school staff, and seen by the outside agency before being entered on to the record.

To assemble information in such detail is clearly going to be a time-consuming activity. It is worth noting that in *Aspects of Secondary Education in England* (1979), the Inspectorate cited record-keeping as one of four factors on which 'the quality of a school's pastoral care was found to depend very heavily'. Significantly, one of the other items was the 'amount of time needed by form and group tutors to carry out their pastoral duties properly'. Record-keeping is a vital component of pastoral care, and an appropriate amount of time should be devoted to it. A measure of the importance attached to this part of the school's activity, in an American school that the author taught in, was the fact that the July salary cheques were paid only on delivery of completed record folders to the 'Head of Guidance'!

Decisions about what should be included on school records address only half the question. The most carefully assembled record card is useless unless it is easily available to the staff, who need to use it as a basis for their educational planning. The following points facilitate that kind of access:

1. *Records should be centrally and securely stored.* To avoid duplication and wasted effort, all records (by careers teachers, pastoral staff, academic staff) should be kept in one folder, and all folders stored centrally in the school office. The folders should be kept in locked filing cabinets, and the key to those cabinets kept by the senior secretary in that office. Ideally a desk, at which teachers consulting the records could work, should be available.

2. *Recorded access.* Although I have argued for more open access to record cards, it seems necessary to signify their importance by having all who consult them sign a 'record consultation sheet', kept by the secretary who has the key. This would reduce the likelihood of improper use of records and also provide information on the use made of records by staff. End-of-year or lengthy entries into a folder occasionally mean a folder will be taken away from the central storage area. This kind of use must be recorded so that no records are lost. In the vast majority of cases no records should be removed from the central storage area. This means that the area must be a congenial place in which to work.

3. *Right of access and associated problems.* Each school should make its own decisions on this difficult issue. The undoubted tendency would be towards open access for all dealing with the child and

for the child's parents. The question of the rights of the 18+ young adult, still in school, towards records on himself is a further complication. Much of the material on school record cards would provide no shock to the subject or his parents – nor should they, since they ought to be factual statements. However, the complex issues of children in physical danger at home, marital discord between parents and the rights of the divorced parent (who does not have custody of the child but retains an interest in his progress) merit specific attention.

When a child is physically at risk in his home, it is usually very difficult to have concrete evidence of that risk. Indeed, if there is evidence, prosecution and/or a care order will ensue. The problem for school records is how to record suspicion in an ethical way. My suggestion is that factual statements (of previous conviction of the parents, of severe injury or bruising received at home) should be recorded on the 'Outside Agencies' report slips, in the normal record card. A special 'Child at Risk' filing system should be kept separately, without the same open access of the normal record system. This set of files would be the responsibility of the head of pastoral care who would decide to whom the information on the card was relevant. Liaison between that responsible teacher and the social services is of crucial importance. The existence of a separate 'Child at Risk' file should be indicted discretely, but clearly, in the child's normal school file.

The importance of the record card emerged clearly in the tragic case of Maria Colwell who died in 1973 as a result of injuries inflicted by her stepfather, who was later convicted of her murder; this conviction was changed, on appeal, to manslaughter. The circumstances surrounding her death led to a DHSS report in 1974, 'Report of the Committee of Inquiry into the Care and Supervision Provided in Relation to Maria Colwell'. Although largely concerned with the social services, the report spends considerable time analysing the role of the education service in this case. Their reason for this was the hope that 'it will be of some general value for the welfare of other school children at emotional or physical risk to analyse this matter in some detail' (p 64). Several cases since that time have highlighted the relevance of the Colwell report for teachers.

The Committee regretted failure to co-ordinate information in the education service, and the lack of liaison between schools and social services. They described 'communication within and between schools' as 'an important link in the welfare chain'. Perhaps, more important, in view of the emphasis the author has laid on keeping records in school, the following severe criticisms were made:

1. After detailing visits by the social worker to the school, the Committee reported: 'None of this was recorded on the card.'
2. Later, when Maria changed schools (she did so twice), 'It is to be noted that this record card at no time showed that there was or had been a care order although the staff ... knew of it.'
3. Further criticism of senior staff appeared: 'In evidence we learned that in the junior school the cards were kept in the school secretary's office. They were not looked at as a matter of routine by the headmaster or deputy. Class teachers were expected to look at them and tell the head, deputy or school secretary anything of importance.'
4. The biting conclusion stated: 'It is reasonable to infer that the staff of the ... *schools did not regard the school record cards as an important part of their record system and preferred to rely in great measure on exchange of information informally*' (author's emphasis).
5. After commenting on the 'false security' offered by unused record cards, the report clearly demonstrated the danger of informal data collection: 'We know that the class teacher in X school was told by (the previous teacher) something of Maria's history. But that teacher left and (a different teacher) had taken over by the time Maria arrived in September, and only some of what was known had been recorded.'

As a consequence of this highly critical report, East Sussex County Council produced 'Children at Risk' (1975), a study which gave recommendations designed to minimise the possibility of the kind of breakdown in communication that led to the death of Maria Colwell. These recommendations are incorporated in the summary below. There is no fail-safe system (subsequent cases of deaths of children show that to be tragically the case) but a greater understanding of the value of the record system reduces the possibility of needles in haystacks.

The question of access to the record cards for an interested (divorced parent without custody) but legally uninvolved party must present problems. There can be no answer for all cases, but the basic principle, the pursuit of the best interests of the child, ought to underlie any discussion on this issue.

The Recommendations of the East Sussex Study (1975)

1. Date and initial all entries.
2. Update the records at least annually.
3. Automatic access for all who share responsibility for the child (special provision for parents of child at risk).
4. Social services should not only have right of access, but should be invited to contribute.
5. Records should move from school to school with the child.
6. A clear distinction should be made between fact and impression. The author's view is that only fact should appear on the school record card – a related 'Child at Risk' file should contain professional impressions of the situation.
7. Record cards, in the majority of cases, do not have the life-or-death implications of the Colwell case. They should, however, be treated with as much professional care as is recommended by the DHSS report.
8. The intention of the record card is to permit the individualisation of each child, so that a properly focused educational provision can be given.
9. The issue of confidentiality is clearly important. Items from record cards should never be the subject of staffroom gossip. Care must be taken to protect the privacy of children and their families from accidental revelation of private material.

A brief case study in four 'acts' follows, as a basis for a discussion by pastoral staff in school. It raises questions which are improtant in record-keeping and will permit staff to share their views on this key aspect of the educational endeavour.

GILLIAN WARREN: A CASE STUDY

Act One

A. 12 years old. Eldest of three children (Philips 6 years, Anne 8 years). The mother died two years before these events occurred and the children continued to live with the father in a three-bedroomed rented terrace property close to the school.
B. The father is an unemployed plumber who supplements his Social Security benefits illegally by doing odd jobs in the neighbourhood. Although the family is by no means comfortably off, the social services are satisfied that the children are adequately cared for. Mr Warren is a regular and heavy drinker.

97

Information A was available to all year tutors and year heads on the cumulative record card kept on each child in the school.

Information B came to light subsequently and is collated from the family caseworker's notes.

On Wednesday, 8 October Gillian arrived at school after being absent on the previous two days. She was bruised about the face and had a note from her father which read as follows:

Dear Sir,
Jill has been off because she fell down the stairs on Sunday night.
P. Warren

Gillian's year tutor, Miss Hunter, received the note during the registration period which preceded each day's work.

Please discuss the following points:

1. What would have been your reaction to Gillian's appearance and note?
2. What is the role of 'data-gathering' in a pastoral system?
3. What methods have you found effective in (a) permitting relevant data to reach appropriate personnel, and (b) maintaining proper ethical standards towards confidential material?
4. What help can your school offer to young teachers given a tutorial responsibility despite minimal training in this aspect of teaching? 'In the context of the child at risk, the class teacher is in an absolutely vital position because he or she sees the child every day it is at school', East Sussex County Council Report *Children at Risk* (1975).

Act Two

Miss Hunter did nothing about the note, and indeed gave little thought to it, accepting it at face value. Some weeks later (at the school-organised Guy Fawkes party) Mr Lewin, Gillian's year head and Miss Hunter's immediate superior, received the following information casually, while chatting with some of his year.

Oh sir, Jill's dad doesn't half bang her if she doesn't get his supper on time. He nearly killed her one night – threw her down the stairs.

He allowed the comment to pass without more ado, but resolved to have a word with the year tutor.

When Mr Lewin asked Miss Hunter to pay careful attention to Gillian Warren, her memory was jogged and she told Mr Lewin of the incident of 8 October. Nothing untoward had happened since then, but Jill's level of work was below the level one would have expected from her NFER test scores. Mr Lewin repeated his recommendation to Miss Hunter that Jill be carefully watched, but that no further action need be taken.

Please discuss the following points:

1. Do you agree with the course recommended by the year head?
2. What other courses of action could he have taken? Why would you accept/reject these possibilities?
3. How much freedom of action would you as a year head have given to a year tutor?

Act Three

The rest of the year passed without further incident, although Gillian's work was still of a very low quality. Miss Hunter expressed her worries about Gillian's social isolation to her year head, but no action was taken apart from efforts made by Miss Hunter to be sympathetic and encouraging to the girl.

The following September, Gillian moved with her class into the third year and to a new year head and tutor. Because much of the foregoing data was anecdotal, little of it found its way on to the child's record card and the new pastoral staff started the year with none of the information about the possible assaults.

Please discuss the following points:

1. How would you ensure adequate information exchange in a horizontal system of pastoral care?
2. What problems in communication are possible in a vertical (house) system? How can they be solved?

Act Four

Shortly before Christmas, in her third year, Gillian, now 13 years old, arrived at school with a badly swollen shoulder, which came to light in a PE lesson. The PE mistress observed considerable bruising in addition to the shoulder injury and, in the investigating conversation with Gillian, the girl broke down, cried and revealed a long history of violent physical assaults by the father against her.

The PE mistress took the information to her head of department, and by this academic route it found its way to the head who had overall responsibility for pastoral care. A more detailed interview with Gillian confirmed the initial information, and the head informed the police and the social services of what had happened.

Please discuss the following points:

1. What strategies can be usefully employed to ensure that relevant, well-based anecdotal information is passed on where appropriate?
2. How can the efforts of academic and pastoral staff be co-ordinated formally?
3. Is the school's responsibility ended when a referral to an outside agency is made?

It is of vital importance to bear in mind that most local authorities now have a clearly set-out procedure for dealing with suspected non-accidental injury. *All staff must be aware of these procedures.* It was, therefore, of great significance that in a brief survey, carried out by the author, of over 30 teachers from several local authorities in 1981, not one knew of the existence of such a procedure. One head, who knew of its existence, had to consult a file to find out what it said. If this case study draws attention to the need to clarify procedures, improve communication and facilitate liaison with the local social services, it will more than justify its existence. It is essential that schools read and implement DES circular 4/88, 6 July and DHSS circular 26/88, 6 July.

More recently (1986–87), the BBC 'Childwatch' telephone service for children suffering abuse from adults suggests that, despite all our efforts, there are still too many needles hidden in school. Helping these needles to make themselves visible, to ask for help, is a major part of our responsibility in facilitating the personal development of our pupils.

Chapter 6

Counselling in School

In an attempt to encourage graduates into the teaching profession, a recent DES publication (*Teaching as a Career*, 1987d) described counselling as involving 'having big ears and nodding at the right time'. It is an astonishingly ignorant statement emanating, one supposes, from the hip, publicity-crazy philosophy which places veneer before substance. It is barely excusable on the grounds that it was intended (one hopes) to be humorous. Throughout this book great emphasis has been given to the complexity of challenges facing teachers. As well as the vast range of learning difficulties present in every classroom, there is the additional parallel task of responding to the bereaved, the pregnant, the substance abuser, the physically and sexually abused, the emotionally immature and the socially incompetent. The largest ears and most synchronised nodding will have minimal impact on such problems, and the implicit suggestion that counselling is a jokey chat strips from teachers an invaluable and effective professional tool.

It is important to mention that the Inspectorate has consistently emphasised the importance of counselling, and the aberration identified above must have given them as much professional pain as it did to teachers and counsellors. There is ample evidence that counselling 'works'; it helps individuals respond to the challenges of life, to grow, to make the most of themselves. Not only do industry, commerce and the public services seek training for their personnel in the skills and abilities involved in counselling, but at times of special stress (the Bradford fire, the Zeebrugge ferry disaster, the King's Cross tube fire) it is increasingly recognised that skilled counselling can help individuals cope in the most difficult circumstances. Given the current complexity of school life, counselling is a service that must be available for both staff and students. Nevertheless, the reality is that the last ten years have seen a decline in the number of counsellors appointed to school, but this decline in specialist appointments has been paralleled by a high increase in numbers of teachers who have enhanced their 'task-competence' skills in subjects to include basic counselling skills. Increasingly, counselling ability is seen as a fundamental professional requirement of the teacher, as well as of managers in other sectors of the professional activity of this country and, as with all such fundamental changes in perception, the quality and depth of training demanded is increasing exponentially. Gone are the days when trainers received requests for a two-day counsellor training course. It is realised that useful though two days are for introducing basic concepts and skills, counsellor training is a much more substantial business. I recently spent some time with students working in the Counselling Psychology Department at Penn State University. A typical profile for counsellor training there involved an initial degree with a considerable psychology component, a one-year Master's programme, a minimum three-year doctoral programme, followed by a one-year supervised internship working as a counselling psychologist. It is light years away from big ears and nodding heads – perhaps we ignore some of the more impressive aspects of the American education system unintentionally. The closest we get to the American experience can be seen where teachers with a first degree (with some psychology) undertake a Master's programme which has a substantial practical component but such courses are still relatively rare in this country. Nevertheless, a rapid excursion through the literature suggests a growing respectability for counselling at the present time (Daws, 1976; DES, 1973; Hamblin, 1974; DES, 1979; Fletcher, 1980; Lang, 1988).

However, one still finds a remarkably durable resistance to it even among many teachers. The feelings of unease, which counselling in school seems to engender, have been outlined with admirable precision by Richardson (1979) whose article, 'Objections to personal counselling in schools', draws together the reservations which have hitherto influenced attitudes to school counselling, without ever having been clearly voiced in this country. Like the Americans, Cicourel and Kitsuse (1963), Richardson identifies a number of specific objections to counselling though, unlike his predecessors, he does confess to an element of methodic, Cartesian doubt in his scepticism. Where Cicourel and Kitsuse make an attack on counselling in school, Richardson issues a challenge – 'justify yourself' – and that challenge must be faced. Richardson presents what he calls a 'strong thesis', that school counselling is so seriously flawed that it must be rejected wholesale, and a 'weak thesis', that certain evident dangers inherent in counselling must be examined and steps taken to minimise them. He offers little support for the strong thesis (indeed, he identifies its 'glaring weakness') but does seem inclined towards the less radical proposal, suggesting that school counsellors keep all options open in an atmosphere of 'disciplined and vigilant hesitation'. It is doubtful that anyone would want to argue against the proposition that counsellors should operate with proper caution and critical awareness, but it would be unfair to dismiss Richardson's challenge on that ground as tautologous. He does, however, present school counsellors with six areas of possible danger in their activity; a brief analysis of counselling from these points of view is worth while.

The danger of labelling children

This is Richardson's first anxiety. While it is certainly the case that some children are labelled as a result of counsellor intervention, the purpose of counselling is the opposite. To criticise counselling on the basis of the effects of bad counselling is as unfair as criticising medicine or education, having observed poor medical practice or bad teaching. What we can gain from Richardson's observation is an awareness of the need for more effective counsellor training and an openness to the possibility of inadequate counselling practice. The counsellor's intention is to help the child shake off previous labelling: 'The end point of any counselling effort is to help the client to become self-sufficient and to minimise his dependence on his physical and social environment' (Brammer and Shostrum, p 72, 1968, 1982). Of course, aims are not always achieved, and so Richardson's worry must also be the counsellor's worry but, if the counsellor has labelled, he has not counselled. Egan (1986) sums up the appropriate value thus: 'The function of helpers is not to remake the lives of their clients, but to help them handle problems in living and refashion their lives according to their own values.'

Counselling infringes civil liberties

This, claims Richardson, occurs by 'subjecting the child to unwanted and damaging surveillance and interference'. By using the word 'damaging', Richardson begs his question. As a parent, I observe my children meticulously; observation (surveillance is a rather loaded word-choice which must cast doubts on the objectivity of this second objection) is a normal, not to say crucial, activity in human interaction (Argyle, 1988). Of course, there is an area of danger here, but the reader is referred to the discussion of appraisal and records in Chapters 4 and 5. One supposes that Richardson could not suggest that we ought not to observe children in school; that he would not ask us not to intervene in their lives. We are again presented with the problem of balance – in this case, balance between help and interference. His related suggestion, that counselling may deflect attention away from the deficiencies of the institution, fails to take into account the increasing influence of ecological and systems approaches to counselling (Blocher, 1974; Minuchin, 1974). The concept of the pathogenic school or family causing problems instead of helping children to solve them (Chapters 1 and 2) is a further example of how, increasingly, the milieu is seen as an important factor in personal development (Rutter *et al.*, 1979; Schostak, 1983).

The individual's right to 'self'

Emphasised by what Richardson calls the 'new romanticism', this is seen as another source of potential disaster, leading children down the road to narcissistic self-contemplation and introspection. Yet, that is one polarity; the other is ignorance of, lack of contact with, distaste for and unfamiliarity with one's self. Counselling is concerned that neither polarity should obtain. Rosenberg (1965) and Burns (1979) are among a host of authors who stress the importance of self-esteem in the individual. Hamblin (1974) uses an analysis of Jahoda to explore the concept 'mental health'. The first of a number of key elements is 'the attitude of the individual towards himself'. One has to conclude that to have an attitude towards oneself involves exploration and evaluation of the self. Once more, Richardson's caveat about excess in no way invalidates counselling activity.

Alienation

The question of alienation – living a life in which we feel powerless, lacking in influence and dignity – is the fourth area Richardson feels counsellors ought to examine carefully. His anxiety here echoes the earlier reservations expressed by Cicourel and Kitsuse (1963), that counselling is an activity that drains initiative from the client and devalues his personal responses to life's challenges, virtually taking over from him the responsibility for his life. When Morris (1972) commented that 'the notion that children and adults can work together as real equals, so far as responsibility is concerned ... is a piece of extremely dangerous self-deception' (p 89), he was pointing out that the greater cognitive, social and emotional maturity of the teacher must be recognised if the teacher–pupil relationship is to be an honest (and therefore productive) one. He was not suggesting that the inequality would lead the teacher to drain away the child's initiative; on the contrary, he saw a productive tension between the regulative and permissive aspects of the teacher–pupil relationship. So it is in counselling. The danger outlined by Richardson, Kitsuse and Cicourel can occur, but that fact no more invalidates appropriate counselling than an authoritarian, constraining, inhibiting teacher invalidates teaching. Counselling seeks to produce the opposite effect from alienation – responsibility for self. Counsellors frequently hear complaints from clients that too great a burden of responsibility for self is placed on them. Perhaps Egan (1975, p 96) sums up the proper counsellor stance on this issue most succinctly: 'Ultimately, if the client chooses to live less effectively than he can, the counsellor obviously should respect his choice.' Self-determination is an ultimate value in counselling.

Counselling skill and professionalism

Richardson's final two concerns are that a mythology about counselling skill and a related veil of professionalisation seek to hide that the emperor counselling has, in fact, no clothes. He is quite properly reminding counsellors that efficacy, some proof of results, ought to be asked for, not only by those who may wish to use counselling services, but also by the practitioners themselves. Do counsellors, in fact, do anything more than the friend who offers a broad shoulder to cry on? Do they have any greater effect than those people who suggest to those in trouble that they should grin and bear it and soldier on? It was certainly the finding of Carkhuff and Berenson (1977) that many counsellors operated at ineffective levels; that some had no effect, and others actually reduced the functionality of clients. However, what Carkhuff and Berenson also revealed was that some counsellors were very effective. It is the analysis of what made them effective which must constitute the second part of this chapter.

However, before leaving the statement of the case against counselling, the author would like to discuss an anxiety he has often heard expressed by teachers. There is a strong feeling among many teachers that the 'permissive' and 'non-directive' emphasis, which dominated much of the literature of the 1960s, would vitiate the proper role of the teacher. As teachers, we feel comfortable in a clear, didactic role; we are trained along that path and feel at home with it. We know that some control and direction is essential for children's cognitive growth, and we suspect that counselling activities will cause us to abdicate that authority and control. Teaching is less ambivalent than counselling; counselling suggests a degree of mutuality and sharing which might well destroy the teaching relationship. Counselling in school is thus rejected as being incompatible with the 'real' task of the school, cognitive development of children.

This is a practical problem, rather than the somewhat theoretical issues identified by Richardson, and it needs to be looked at carefully. It is unfortunate that the two words 'permissive' and 'non-directive' have become so interwoven with the idea of counselling. They have overtones of an abdication of responsibility which quite rightly makes the school pause. In fact, they were initially used, with a very limited, precise meaning, to describe the kind of atmosphere within which a client could be expected to identify his own difficulties. Clients were seen as needing that kind of freedom to explore themselves, rather than have an influential, directive judge telling them who they were from the outside. Great skill is needed in using non-directive techniques, but these by no means constitute the full range of counsellor skills. As we shall see later in the chapter, counsellors do take initiatives, do direct and do share their judgement of situations with the client. Exploration of 'who' and 'where' I am is one phase of counselling, often best achieved using 'non-directive' techniques.

So much for the anxieties of those who oppose counselling in school. No counsellor would wish to defend the activities and inadequacies identified by Richardson, nor would any counsellor feel able to accept the charge that he turned away from his responsibilities in dealing with young people. Conformity in pupils, invasion of privacy, pampering or warping the self-concept and neglecting responsibility, are the antithesis of what counselling should be about. Education in general and counselling in particular aim to produce divergence of thought, respect for the desire for privacy, the development of self-reliance and decision-making ability, and a sense of security from which critical, analytical skills can tackle the problems facing late twentieth-century man. The purpose of developing self-awareness is not to satisfy a narcissistic need to contemplate oneself in a favourable light, but because incontrovertible psychological evidence associates a favourable self-concept with the ability to turn outwards in a constructive manner (see Rosenthal and Jacobson, 1966; Rogers, 1967; Insell and Jacobson, 1977; Burns, 1979). The question remains: 'Is counselling a proper activity in school?' So far all we have is a consistent, but not particularly reassuring, statement that what Richardson and others worry about is not counselling. A more positive statement is needed: 'What is counselling, how effective can it be, and what is the best way of deploying counselling skills in school?'

What is counselling?

One of the great difficulties in any discussion of counselling is that it is a multi-dimensional concept. Its very breadth makes it too easy for individuals to talk at cross-purposes, one person attacking a view that the other has not proposed simply because each means something different by the word 'counselling'. Although the word is widely used today, few people when pressed are able to say precisely what they mean by it. One definition, which takes into account the range of helping relationships which exist from simple, sympathetic listening to deep psychotherapy, is: 'Counselling involves the use of a wide range of skills within the context of a relationship whose characteristics create for the client an environment of such safety, respect and support that he finds it possible to take the risks involved in independence and creative response to life's challenges.' Where ten years ago students were expelled or suspended, now they are 'counselled out'; phenomena like 'tickle and scream' therapy add what seems to be a humorous dimension to discussions about counselling; respected university colleagues can refer to group work disparagingly as 'grope work' – little wonder that the counsellor is still struggling for a toe hold among his educational colleagues. Perhaps the most effective way forward is to expand that definitional groundwork, which I propose to do briefly along two lines. Each looks at counselling from a different viewpoint.

PROCESS OF THE COUNSELLING RELATIONSHIP

At the risk of over-simplifying, we can say that counselling takes place in three basic phases: an exploratory phase in which the client is helped to view himself and his difficulties less rigidly by loosening blocks that prevent influential perceptions from being examined; an understanding phase in which the client is helped to structure his new, less rigid, more open perceptions of reality in a way that gives him greater control over himself and his environment; an action phase in which specific plans to expand his coping repertoire are developed so that functionality is increased.

These three phases do not necessarily follow a rigid chronological sequence; indeed, overlap between them is to be expected, so that exploration and understanding will develop together, and plans for action will exist in embryo form while understanding is growing. Before looking in more detail at each phase, it is pertinent to add a comment about the counselling relationship. The idea of sending someone for counselling, or imposing it on them, is a contradiction – whatever the relationship is when we send one person to another, it is not counselling. That is not to devalue, for example, a disciplinary interview; it is simply to distinguish unequivocally a disciplinary and a counselling role.

The topics which appear as the focus of a counselling interview are as varied as human activity: job problems; teenage sexuality; parental rejection; feelings of inadequacy; loneliness; worries about religion; inadequate social skills; aggressiveness; timidity; and so on. Counsellors often find that the 'presenting problem' – the issue initially exposed to the counsellor – is simply a means of establishing contact and testing out how trustworthy, shockable or helpful the counsellor is. The presenting problem can mask something which is causing greater anxiety but whose revelation is at that time too taxing.

Let us look in a little more detail at the phases of counselling. No book can teach people to counsel any more than it can teach people to play golf or do surgery. Counselling is a sophisticated practical skill with a well-established theoretical base: I propose to outline selections from that theoretical base and describe some items of practice; the purpose of the description is to provide illustration, not training.

Exploration

One of the nicer compliments we pay people is when we say 'he is a good listener'. It is a compliment which identifies in him that high degree of unselfishness which puts the 'listened to' person on top priority. My agenda, my interests, my preoccupations, when I am *really* listening, become totally secondary to the other person's agenda, interests, preoccupations. Thus questions (ie what interests me) can become intrusive sidetracks which divert the listened-to person from *his* concerns. In one exercise designed to sensitise trainee counsellors to the difficulty of total listening, a group of 12 is invited to 'listen' to one of its members. That member is invited to present something important to the group, and the group is invited to respond in a way that helps that member explore his theme. Thus on one occasion the exchange was as follows:

Well ... it's not very much really – but I suppose I'd like to talk about the birth of my first child.

Response 1: 'Were you present at the birth?'
Response 2: 'Was it a long labour?'
Response 3: 'Was the baby born in hospital?'

Response 4: 'Was it a boy or a girl?'
Response 5: 'Did your wife have an epidural?'

Despite all our discussions, the listening had become an interrogation – sympathetic, interested, supportive, but nevertheless it was the *group's* agenda, not the client's. The questions were the interests of the group, not necessarily or centrally those of the client. We were exploring *our* interests, not helping the client explore his concerns. Then:

Response 6: 'I was puzzled that you said the birth of your first child wasn't "very much really"!'

A statement, not a question. The client's agenda not mine. And the client replied, 'Well ... I suppose I said that because the baby died.' Not one of the questions elicited that key piece of information, but by staying with the client's agenda, one group member made it possible for him to share that fact. Carl Rogers, who has contributed vastly to our understanding of the importance of leaving our client free to follow his agenda (1942; 1962; 1965), has described a technique often called reflecting, which he saw as something more than a mirroring activity. The essence of it is when a client entrusts the counsellor with some comment like, 'I am feeling very, very down in the dumps'. The counsellor can then block exploration and understanding of that feeling by offering an intrusive, interpretive comment like, 'Perhaps it's the time of the month' (ie, don't worry, it's normal), or 'We all feel like that now and again. We've just got to grin and bear it' (ie don't exaggerate, you're not unusual).

If the response reflects accurately the client's feeling – 'The whole world is looking black and gloomy, eh?' – there is no intrusion. The statement here is, 'Okay, I'm with you – where do you want to go now?' If the client is to arrive at real self-awareness, the counsellor needs to remain supportive but not intrusive. Rogers (1965) describes the counsellor's role thus:

Rather than serving as a mirror, the therapist becomes a companion to the client as the latter searches through a tangled forest in the dead of night. The therapist's responses are more in the nature of calls through the darkness: 'Am I with you?', 'Is this where you are?', 'Are we together?'. (pp 112–13)

It is inordinately difficult to adopt this role; the temptation to give the benefit of our experience, our perceptions and our understanding to the client is almost overpowering, but it must be resisted if we are to be able to counsel. The questions we may want to ask may be important, interesting – to us. But, at least in the exploratory stage, we need to give the client maximum freedom to explore where he wants to go. The aim of this part of the counselling process is to allow the client to get to the point of saying with confidence, 'This is the difficulty, this is my concern, my worry.' It involves a recognition on our part that the presenting problem may not be the real problem – and the client needs space and support if the real problem is to be identified. Thus a presenting problem of poor work may in reality be the problem of being bullied; misbehaviour may involve difficulty at home; difficulties about career prospects and higher education may really be about financial difficulties for the family. Failure to permit a genuine exploratory phase will leave the counsellor chewing away at the pseudo-issue and the client diverted from his real concern.

Understanding

Rigidity of perception affects us all to some degree, since none of us can see 'all of the possibilities'. Some people, however, see so few of the possibilities that room for manoeuvre in their life becomes very limited. They become increasingly constrained until eventually there appears to be no way to turn and anxiety and distress increase. Problem-solving is really the identification of as wide a range of possibilities as possible, and the ability to evaluate those various possibilities. Solving problems which face us in life is no different and, most of the time, most of us do a fair job of identifying and evaluating possible actions which would lessen our stress. When that wider perception seems to escape someone, a counsellor can help him to find it.

The modern media have made us all familiar with the dramatic visual tricks that Gestalt psychologists can play with our perception. We can see in Figure 6.1 either two faces looking at each other or a goblet. We can become fixed in one perception or the other, or we may be able at will to alter field and ground to see whichever picture we prefer. The same applies to the picture of the bearded man who hides a naked lady in his features.

Just as our perception of external objects can be limited, rigidified and static, so our perception of ourselves, our problems and our situation can be so rigid as to make movement and change very difficult. The counsellor has to try to help his client make the same kind of perceptual shift internally that externally allows us to see first faces, then goblet, first man, then naked lady. How might that be achieved?

When the client is able to identify clearly his area of concern, then,

Figure 6.1. *Rigidity/fluidity of perception*

using approaches developed by Friedrick Perls (1973), the counsellor can begin to help the client loosen the limiting, uni-dimensional perspective through which the problem is being viewed. At the risk of vastly over-simplifying the profound thinking of Perls, we might usefully consider one technique for lessening rigidity of perception which is developed from his work.

George was disruptive in a naughty rather than a malicious way, but so constantly that his school was at its wits' end about what to do next. Punishment of all kinds had been meted out but with no apparent effect; George had been bawled out, cajoled, reprimanded, put into detention, separated from his class, yet still his temper tantrums, petty vandalism and insolence continued. Eventually, after a chat with the school counsellor, they agreed to try the following Gestalt approach.

Two chairs were placed two yards apart, facing each other. George was asked to sit on one chair, facing the other empty seat. The counsellor stood near, as unobtrusively as possible.

George, I want you to imagine that Mr Galton (the headmaster) is sitting in that chair. Will you tell him what you think about his school?

Initially suspicious, George soon warmed to his task, half surprised by the liberal invitation, half enjoying it. He spoke for about two minutes, outlining his perception of the school, as oppressive, anti-child, having favourites, being prejudiced. As soon as the initial flood of hostility and negative feeling dried up, the counsellor interjected:

> Sit on the other chair. You are now Mr Galton. Can you see George Daley in the chair opposite? Try to tell him what you, as headmaster, see when you look at him.

George was less sure here, but made an attempt to look at himself through his headteacher's eyes. He said he saw 'an idiot' and 'a layabout'. He was much less comfortable being squeezed into a different perceptual framework, but made a real effort to make the shift. Again when he fell silent, the counsellor intervened:

> You are George Daley. Sit in your own chair. You've heard what Mr Galton thinks of you. What do you say to that? Are you an idiot? A layabout?

George now found himself being pushed into a degree of self-analysis and self-justification that he had never tried before. He explained that his idiotic behaviour was in some ways a response to peer expectation and, in others, a statement of disenchantment with what was going on in school for him. From the point of view of my illustration, the salient feature is that George was able, very quickly, to fall in with a role-play that vastly expanded his perceptual horizons; an internal debate had been established, a willingness to see a different point of view, other possible outcomes and behaviour.

The counsellor manages the situation, but must be meticulous in avoiding the trap of putting his perceptions into the situation. He will add chairs for other characters if he thinks it necessary, thus altering the perspective, or he may offer a clarifying comment or ask for some clarification from the client. This is no panacea but rather a small example of one technique which can be used in the initial phase of exploration. Clearly, as exploration continues, and more fluid perception of reality occurs, then understanding will be under way. I have used this technique with success in a wide range of problems; school counsellors may well be attracted by the speed with which it allows exploration to get under way. Further details about this approach will be found in the work of Perls, and many organisations now offer courses which have in them practical work based on Gestalt approaches (consult the British Association for Counselling Register).

Once rigidity in the way in which a client perceives himself and his situation is loosened, the possibility of understanding the problem being faced becomes possible. Different counsellors use a host of theoretical positions to explain why we behave as we do: the influence of repressed infantile experience; significant occurrences in childhood; damage to or lack of self-esteem; lack of cognitive skill and decision-making ability; or absence of contact with our own influential attitudes and feelings. In one sense, the direction from which a counsellor comes theoretically is less important than his skill in helping the client to formulate his own hypothesis in a way which will allow greater functionality and less stress to occur. Brammer and Shostrum (1976, p 75) emphasise that the key to effective counselling lies in helping the client to come more fully into contact with his environment:

> We feel that one reason people err in judgement is that they include data which do not belong to the present context and exclude data which do. Thus people who exclude data from their present situation and react only in terms of memories and stereotypes from previous learnings, as if this were reality, are in trouble ... Or, conversely, people who react to present situations without the benefit of past experiences which may be locked via repression deep within the unconscious core system, may be in trouble as well.

Their argument is that our understanding of reality (and consequently our evaluation of current difficulties and possible solutions) is distorted and even destroyed when our experience is used selectively. Thus, a teenage boy with whom I worked had selectively used his experience to arrive at a low, undemanding self-image. He had constantly to distort any new positive experience to fit in with his well-established, comfortable, but destructive, self-view. When a teacher complimented his work, or a friend described him in favourable terms, he felt obliged to re-cast what he had experienced in a way which left his poor self-image intact:

> Mr Jones always tries to buck people up, even if they're no good. He just tries to keep you going.

The understanding phase tries to bring the client face to face with the distortions, encouraging him to explore why such distortions are necessary. It is vital that the counsellor should not intrude on what must be a personal understanding for the client. Suggestions by the counsellor to the client simply offer an external perception; what must occur is that the client should be helped to move forward towards understanding himself in his own terms. Easy to say – very difficult to achieve. (Can the counsellor draw discrepant perceptions of reality into the open in a way that permits the client to arrive at self-understanding?) The task in this 'understanding' phase of counselling is to permit the client to see the presenting problem (identified in the 'exploratory' phase) in its full context, to generate a range of possible responses, to draw discrepant perceptions of reality into the guessing, so that with all the pieces of the jigsaw on the table, the client can say, 'This is my difficulty, the challenge I face, and this is what I want to do about it.'

As a series of counselling interviews occurs, a deepening willingness to explore and a greater capacity for understanding the self will appear in the client. Events from earlier years, current feelings, old stereotypes and beliefs long thought to be rejected but still influential will emerge to complete a jigsaw in which the problem will be seen as increasingly 'understandable'. There is a degree of comfort in that alone, but the third phase of counselling tries to go beyond that by increasing living skills; it is action focused.

Action

The client may well have decided that he needs to change his way of behaving in the light of new understanding of his situation. George, the disruptive who explored his reality in the Gestalt approach, may now know why he is naughty, may see that other possibilities exist, will have looked at the long-term consequences of his behaviour and may want to change. However, this is something which will be very difficult since expectations among his teachers and friends have been firmly established. He himself will be almost programmed to respond in disruptive ways in certain situations. What then can the counsellor offer in planning some effective action for him? Krumboltz and Thoresen (1976) have emphasised that effective counselling must produce changes in behaviour. If it does not, then however agreeable the encounter, in their view time has been wasted. Theirs is a behavioural approach which accepts the position of behavioural psychology that actions which result in pleasure for the doer will be repeated, actions which allow the doer to avoid punishment will be repeated, and actions which result in either loss of pleasure or in pain for the doer will not be repeated. Before I am pounced on by both sides in the corporal punishment debate, it is important to add that by far the most effective modifier of behaviour is reward and that the evidence indicates that inflicting pain is a very short-term modifier of behaviour (witness the way in which the same names appear with great regularity in school punishment books). here is an example offered by Krumboltz and Thoresen:

Suppose that we want a child to learn to speak the truth. We must then be sure that speaking the truth is rewarded and that telling lies is not rewarded. Unfortunately the experience of many people is just the opposite. The child who admits transgression is punished immediately, whereas the child who denies the transgression avoids punishment ... we could say to the child: 'Thanks for admitting that you broke the vase. I know that it is hard for you to say so. You've shown a lot of courage. Later on when you're feeling a little better let's talk about some ways that we can arrange for you to replace the vase.' A response like this one provides immediate reinforcement for telling the truth and delays the more aversive consequences of repairing the damage. (p 7)

The broken vase could in fact be any incident in which a child may feel ambiguous about accepting responsibility for his actions, and the general point that Krumboltz wishes to emphasise is that, as a matter of course, desirable behaviour in children ought to be greeted with praise and recognition. The systematisation of this approach is achieved in setting up a behavioural modification programme – one technique which is useful in helping a client expand his coping repertoire. Macmillan and Kolvin (1977) have given an admirable summary of this approach, with special emphasis on teachers' needs. Care is needed in setting up the programme so that success can be seen clearly both by the client and the teacher. Five major areas need to be considered.

1. Define, very precisely, the behaviour to be modified. It is not sufficient to speak of 'disruptive behaviour' or 'constant naughtiness' – these are evaluations of behaviour. What must be looked at is the actual behaviour – shouting out in class, swearing, punching other pupils etc. Then a specific goal needs to be expressed, initially to reduce and ultimately to eradicate George's swearing in class.
2. The environment perspective must be analysed if we are to have a complete database. Where does the swearing occur, with which teachers, in what specific circumstances? What seems to be the pay-off for the child? It is often surprising that careful analysis of this kind reveals that 'constant' misbehaviour in fact occurs in very clearly defined situations.
3. In a sense, the counselling interview is artificial – the action phase needs to take place in real-life settings. Thus disruptive classroom behaviour is solved in the classroom. Once the milieu in which the misbehaviour occurs has been determined, an attempt at modifying it can occur.

4. Behaviour modification uses the principle that people do things because they get some pleasure from them. Thus it is important to discover what pay-off the child is getting (peer approval, evident apoplectic fury of the teacher, being sent out of the room etc) and remove that pay-off. In using behaviour modification I would usually share with the client a simple theoretical explanation of what we could do, enlisting his help in setting up the database and identifying the pay-off.

In addition to removing the pay-off, for the behaviour to be eradicated, it is most effective to plan rewards for desired behaviour. Thus after a disruptive free session George might be allowed to perform some task he enjoys – helping the PE department prepare for a gymnastic display or putting up Christmas decorations. It is quite difficult to identify a suitable reward since often what we see as rewarding an adolescent might hate! This needs careful thought and the help of the pupil in question.

A further problem is that the social aspect of behaviour is often very difficult to control. The peer group may continue to reinforce disruptive behaviour, or another teacher may fail to remove pay-off for the bad behaviour consistently. However, with the pupil's permission, the peer group will often enter into an 'experimental' contract – 'let's see if we can help George stop ...'. The other members of staff need to be committed to the course of action planned by the counselling teacher (cf the notes on case conferences in Chapter 2).

5. Finally, it is important to evaluate the extent to which desired behaviour is established. This reinforces both the teacher and the pupil. It is my experience that, despite initial scepticism, teachers are quite surprised at the effectiveness of this technique. I must stress that, from a counsellor's point of view, this type of modification would follow exploration and understanding of the undesirable behaviour and agreement by the pupil to use the technique. It is a response to the 'I-would-like-to-change-but-don't-think-I-can' reservation often posed by clients.

Again it is important to bear in mind that what appears in the preceding pages is a broad description of the counselling process. In each of the major stages – exploration, understanding and action – a host of strategies and interventions can be used. The Bibliography at the end of this book will identify sources for further information, but I would like to emphasise that counselling skill cannot be acquired from books. I hope that I have indicated what are appropriate aims and what might be achieved in terms of process in school counselling.

Unfortunately, the complication does not end here. As I suggested at the beginning of the chapter, counselling is a multi-dimensional concept. So far we have considered process. Let us move on to a much more important and influential dimension – the quality of the counselling relationship.

QUALITY OF THE COUNSELLING RELATIONSHIP

There is strong evidence to suggest that, however carefully a counsellor follows the stages outlined in the process analysis in terms of outcome, cure or improvement, other more influential factors appear.

Eysenck (1953) made a stinging attack on the efficacy of 'the talking cure', and was at least instrumental in making counsellors and their therapist colleagues take an evaluative pause for breath. By the mid-1960s, Truax and Carkhuff (1967) were able to present a re-analysis of the data and concluded:

> Eysenck was essentially correct in saying that average counselling and psychotherapy as it is currently practised does not result in average client improvement greater than that observed in clients who received no special counselling or psychotherapeutic treatment. (p 5)

In other words, clients improved just as quickly whether they were counselled or not; counselling appeared to be a neutral, ineffective activity. The important extension of Eysenck's findings by Truax and Carkhuff (their work is developed later by Carkhuff and Berenson [1977]) was that some counsellors did produce significant beneficial results.

The inexorable logic of that presents us with a disturbing conclusion. If, on average, counselling has the same result as no treatment, and if some counsellors do produce results better than the spontaneous, untreated recovery rate, some counsellors must be retarding or preventing improvement. This finding needs to be emphasised, since it explains to some extent the reservations culled from Richardson at the beginning of this chapter. Counselling can harm as well as help and it is important that anyone involved in counselling is aware that he can do harm as well as good. An obvious response to those findings is to analyse carefully the counselling techniques of those counsellors who were consistently successful to try to identify what qualities and skills they brought to their activity which were absent in the unsuccessful counsellors. Carkhuff and Berenson (1977) presented such an analysis of what are now called 'core dimensions' – the specific qualities of those counsellors who consistently facilitated beneficial change in their clients. They comment:

> In counselling and therapy, teacher–student or parent–child relationships, the consequences may have constructive or deteriorative effects on intellectual and physical as well as emotional functioning.

They go on to show that the facilitative or retarding effect correlates with the presence or absence of 'a core of dimensions that are shared by all interactive processes'. The general finding (Brammer and Shostrum, 1982) that all schools of thought produce results in counselling seems to support the view that techniques and underlying theories are less influential on effect than the *quality of the relationship* within which those techniques are used which, of course, takes us back to Chapters 2 and 3.

The core dimensions identified by the American research are:

1. The ability to empathise, ie an ability to allow oneself as counsellor to experience or merge with the experience of the client, reflecting on that experience while suspending one's own judgements, and communicating this to the client. It involves an ability to be where the client is, without becoming tangled in the rigid perceptions that the client brings to the relationship. Thus a teacher who said to me, 'There's no way I can think like a teenager', may well have been saying he could not usefully engage in counselling. Advice-giving, support, guidance, perhaps, but not counselling.

2. Unconditional positive regard, ie an ability to communicate to the client a level of human warmth, commitment to help, willingness to try to understand, which indicates a clear statement that the client is highly valued by the counsellor. While it is useful to bear in mind Waskow's (1963) comment, that respect can be communicated via anger, it is clear that anger that lacks fundamental respect for the client cannot be facilitative. A pertinent exchange, which negatively illustrates this concept, occurred during a question following a talk I gave recently: 'You made much in your lecture of the personal dignity and worth of children. What about those children who don't have any personal dignity or worth?' Such a teacher might achieve excellent exam results, exemplary classroom order, but he is unlikely to counsel effectively.

3. Genuineness, ie the ability to establish a relationship with the client in which there is no, or minimal, conflict between one's total experience and awareness and one's overt communication with the client. The relationship should be characterised by honesty and openness, rather than exploitation and manipulation. Again, talking recently about the problems and worries youngsters have about unemployment, one teacher remarked, 'We can't tell them the truth about it. All we can do is tell them lies to keep the lid on.'

I would be the last to suggest that the three teachers' negative comments are typical, but they do illustrate effectively the kind of interaction which all the evidence suggests is counter-productive. It is that type of relationship which, according to the new extensive research findings, reduces the chances of a client coming to terms with himself and his difficulties.

Counselling and pastoral care

The foregoing has deliberately suggested that counselling is a skilled activity, with real potential for harm if it is practised by the unskilled and the untrained. It may seem to be a negative statement, but I feel it is vital that we escape the notion that counselling is little more than a sympathetic chat, the 'Big-Ears and Noddy' syndrome. At the same time I would like to propose that it is an essential ingredient in the guidance services offered in pastoral care. We have a dilemma and the possible solution is to look again at the multi-dimensional aspect of counselling. The 'friendly barmaid' style of counselling is one which many people see as the paradigm. 'Get it off your chest, have a good cry, dear', and then, 'There, you feel better now, don't you?' The aim, though rarely articulated, is to offer sympathetic support in a transitory, non-judgemental way, and it does seem to work. People do go away feeling better. It is not that that style of human relationship is wrong; rather, it is a holding operation. Little growth or movement will take place, but there will often be greater comfort and ease, at least for a time.

People who can effectively offer that kind of relationship are quite rightly highly valued by their colleagues and friends – they help people to keep going. A pastoral care system requires these qualities as basic attributes of its personnel. It is a starting point, and an extremely valuable one.

All teachers know that schools do have to cope with mentally ill children (Jones, 1975) and that they are expected to cope while a referral is being negotiated. Our role with such disturbed children is akin to that of a man with some degree of first aid awaiting the arrival of a doctor to treat a seriously injured man. We have to ensure, as far as possible, the comfort of the patient, reduce his anxiety and prevent further injury. So it is when teachers face such troubled children – and the skills which permit them to operate at the left-hand side of the continuum (see Figure 6.2) are invaluable in such circumstances. That said, there is enormous scope for the development of the counselling skills on the right-hand side of the continuum. Hopson and Scally (1979) make the following pertinent comment:

> As far as counselling is concerned there are reasons to regard Britain as an under-developed country. The ratio of specialist counsellors to client population here is probably similar to the doctor–patient ratio in many Third World countries. With the realisation that specialist availability at present is barely existent and that training resources are currently being cut back, the implication is that training ought to be towards producing the counselling equivalent of paramedics.

The move in this direction has already begun in the USA. Kanfer and Goldstein (1975) hold a carefully argued position on helping what they call 'paraprofessionals' in counselling techniques. This seems to be the direction in which to go. Short courses of an uncompromisingly practical nature on counselling skills are becoming more common. With the vast majority of teachers becoming increasingly involved in counselling, the availability of such courses must increase. In addition, one-year or two-year Master's courses which had begun to develop in the 1960s and 1970s must be used to expand the numbers of trainer counselling teachers available in schools.

Friendly, chatting, sympathetic support	Counselling growth, facilitation
It is comfortable, non-dynamic, advises, suggests (danger of dependence)	It challenges, is painful, dynamic, facilitates, unblocks (requires independence)

Figure 6.2. *A human interaction continuum*

Perhaps the arrival of school counsellors in the 1960s occurred at a time when schools were uncertain about how to use them. Now that the recognition of their skills is greater, we find that financial constraints make their appointment unlikely. So, to respond to an increasingly obvious gap in our educational provision, teachers need to expand their counselling skills beyond the provision of mere 'support' strategies. Certainly in the interim period we need to maximise our support skills and, where appropriate, refer children with major difficulties.

One strategy which has been used effectively by some universities is for a trained counsellor to work as leader of a support group with local teachers; thus the teachers explore together cases brought by the teachers from their schools. Working with their consultant, the teachers have what is both a training session for themselves and a consultancy service which is beneficial to the pupils they discuss.

I have stressed in this chapter that one cannot learn how to counsel from a book. What I would hope the reader would gain from it is an awareness that counselling has a crucial role to play in school guidance, that it is a highly skilled activity and that teachers can develop those skills. I would inevitably be selective if I suggested training centres where the paraprofessional skills, mentioned by Hopson and Scally, might be developed, but local universities, polytechnics and institutes of higher and further education are obvious first ports of call.

The Bibliography at the end of the book tries to emphasise books of a practical nature, but even they are intended for use in a training situation. The reader should read Egan (1986); Kanfer and Goldstein (1975); Krumboltz and Thoresen (1976); Macmillan and Kolvin (1977); and Keat (1979) which are all books of a practical nature, but they too are intended for use in a training situation. However, they do emphasise both the highly professional approach necessary and the essentially practical nature of counselling.

Chapter 7

Decisions, Decisions – Balancing Pupil Independence with Teachers' Responsibilities

Whether counselling is simply supportive or genuinely growth-enhancing, it is important that the pupil should not become dependent. As we have seen in the previous chapter, one of the major aims of counselling is that it should help children take full responsibility for themselves; it should prepare them to take decisions. It could be argued that the major characteristic of our age is that we are all thrust into choosing – the one thing we cannot choose is not to choose. Even 100 years ago it was much easier to know what one's life would be like ten years later – where one would live, one's job, one's food, clothing, one's sexual life, sport and leisure. All was then much more stable, much less demanding in terms of choice. The Toffler classic (1971) has documented the explosion of choice that faces us as consumers, but we face an equal and perhaps psychologically more taxing range of options in our personal lives. Anxiety is an inevitable corollary of such choice.

In the 1950s Mead concluded her study of Samoan society thus:

> We pay heavily for our heterogeneous, rapidly changing civilisation. We pay in high proportions of crime and delinquency, we pay in the conflicts of youth, we pay in an ever-increasing number of neuroses. (p 169)

It must be a source of some concern to educators that her remarks remain as true today as they were 40 years ago. Her contrasting of the simple lives of the Samoan girls she had been studying with the complex, confusing, choice-full lives of their western counterparts led to a final comment:

> We must turn all our educational efforts to training our children for the choices which confront them.

The question of choice and its coping corollary, decision-making, are constantly discussed by a wide range of authors dealing with the question of healthy survival in our society. Gelatt (1962) asked if the skill is taught in a sufficiently structured and professional manner; Kellmer-Pringle (1965) reminded us that a degree of security and self-confidence need to be established if individuals are to choose effectively; Moore (1970) identified the development of decision-making skills as a key feature of guidance service in schools; Toffler (1971) exposed the enormity of choice that faces late twentieth-century man; and Law and Watts (1977) took us back to the development of decision-making skills in school, preparing us for the organised focus on this area in TVEI and GCSE. There is a powerful concensus that the school curriculum ought, as a priority, to help children develop decision-making skills.

The previous chapter, in discussing counselling, insisted that counselling ceased when a client lost control of his decision-making ability. A provocative parallel statement might be made, that where children lose access to decision-making and are not offered opportunities to develop the skill, education no longer occurs. Of course, one needs to select with care the parameters within which choices can be made, taking into account the age, maturity and confidence of the children. The arguments for and against the wearing of uniform (an interesting word for educators to ponder on!) have been made and we have all shared in the debate. Nevertheless, it has always struck me as singularly incongruous that 16-year-old adults should not be allowed to decide the colour of their sweater as they stand on the threshold of the adult world. Whatever the practical arguments are, one must ask what hidden message an adolescent picks up when he is exhorted to be responsible yet finds himself constrained in so many petty ways.

I suspect that the issue is not one of whether to give responsibility to children, but rather where to draw the line, deciding what are and what are not appropriate areas wherein children might be allowed to decide for themselves, and working out safe but challenging ways in which children can go through the process of decision-making. I would like to work out that issue from two points of view: first, that of the school as an organisation and, second, that of the classroom which is the work situation for pupils for most of the day.

School ethos and decision-making

I have mentioned to colleagues in this country a school I visited in the USA where the pupils interviewed prospective teachers in their school. The practice is consistently viewed with horror, yet the reality was quite impressive. Courteous representatives of different forms in the school posed questions (real ones from the children's point of view and therefore important) to the prospective teachers. It was a serious business, taken seriously by all. In my view, quite ethically the pupils took no part in the final decision, and withdrew from the interview when their questions were answered. The important point was that they were seen as worth-while contributors by the school staff. I submit that it is not unreasonable for pupils' views to be considered in such a situation. I am sure there is no possibility of this practice occurring in this country in the immediate future, though a logical extension of the recent legislation on school governing bodies could be to include pupil representation. If we really want young people to mature, we must give them responsibility.

My own school in Chicago was less adventurous than that, but it did have an active student council which sent representatives to some parts of staff meetings. I invariably found their contributions apposite and constructive. Of course, there are schools in the United Kingdom where pupils are given wide responsibility, but they are undoubtedly exceptional. The consensus of opinion of those involved in such schemes seems to be that the pupils respond in a most mature way to such developed responsibilities.

School ethos has become an in-word with educationalists in the 1980s, but we should not neglect to consider it just for that reason. The concept is not new, it is simply that Rutter's (Rutter *et al.*, 1979) careful analysis of a group of 12 schools offers detailed data on organisational behaviour of schools, with juxtaposed information on the results of those schools in terms of delinquency, pupil behaviour, academic outcome and attendance. He is unequivocal in stating that the findings suggest that:

> Schools in which a high proportion of children held some kind of position of responsibility in the school system had better outcomes with respect to both pupil behaviour and examination success. (p 197)

Rutter's book will undoubtedly have a strong influence on educational practice for many years to come. It offers empirical support for teaching practices which have often been recommended as philosophically sound (dignity of the pupils, non-authoritarian, shared responsibility) but practically destructive of good order. In fact, the contrary is the case. Children do better when they have opportunities to make decisions.

At school level, then, it seems that involving the pupils in the system produces beneficial results in terms of behaviour and academic performance. Thus, pupil councils, clubs which have pupil officers and questionnaire consultations of pupils are all structural statements about a school's ethos. Of course, much more influential is the day-to-day interaction between staff and pupils. If it is known among the pupils that the outward show of consultation is sham, no amount of that pretence will produce the desired effect. As in so many of the potentially productive elements of school life, we find that staff attitude is the key issue. It is not inappropriate to add that Rutter found that teachers too like to feel they have some part in the decision-making process; the same caveats about pretence need to be considered by senior management in school. It is astonishing that some headteachers feel it appropriate to decide not only on pupil dress, but on whether or not their women members of staff may wear trousers.

Decision-making in the classroom

The general statements about ethos in school can be made about individual classrooms. Individual teachers make implicit statements to their pupils about their work just as whole staff do on an institutional level. As a class teacher I might usefully ask myself how my pupils' decision-making skills are developed (or retarded?) in my classroom. Do they make any decisions? Do I share with them the process by which I have arrived at my decisions? Do my decisions appear arbitrary, capricious or merely accidental to them? Undoubtedly, part of learning to make decisions occurs as a result of seeing other competent decision-makers operate. What kind of a model am I? Perhaps a helpful approach here would be to look at some specific ways in which children might be helped at classroom level to develop decision-making skills. Gelatt (1962) offers an initial theoretical framework by saying that decision-making involves:

1. A clear definition of the problem to be considered.
2. A collection of data which is analysed in the light of the problem.
3. A study of what possibililties exist.
4. An evaluative analysis of the consequences of each possible alternative.
5. A decision based on the above.

Thus, in a classroom, pupils can be invited to identify the nub of an issue (it can be academic, social, personal, to do with values, relationships etc), collect data they regard as relevant to the problem, work out and discuss likely results in terms of possible, probable and desirable outcomes, eventually arriving at a considered decision. They can be asked to analyse both facts and values, take account of logical analysis and have an awareness of personal philosophies.

This structural approach to problem-solving contrasts starkly with the caprice that often governs adolescent problem-solving, and is best viewed as a skill to be developed for use in real-life situations. It can be used across the full range of adolescent experiences, and needs a skilful leader whose task will be to use the problem-solving exercise to develop all the broad aims of guidance, plus the important skill of structured attack on problems.

Gelatt emphasises that this approach is 'heuristic', not simply logical (p 241). It contrasts with the simply logical emphasis in the CRAC series *Your Choice* (1971–74). This series examined vocational problems, but on an abstract, logical level. Data was given, but the manipulation of the data was at a hypothetical level. To use the heuristic approach recommended by Gelatt would involve simulated reality; for example, an invitation to one pupil to explain (using carefully collected, relevant data) to his parents, housemaster, prospective employer, friends, why he proposed leaving school at 16 despite the academic ability to stay on for further study. The use of simulation exercises has become well established in industry and commerce, but strangely education has been slow to see their value. The time-worn adage (which in my youth constituted the basis for a method lecture for student teachers) says most succinctly what the real value of simulation is: I hear and I forget; I see and I remember; I do and I understand. Even simulated 'doing' offers a potential for probing decision-making which cannot be matched except by the real thing.

> Simulation takes those who take part out of the role of spectator and moves them into the role of player. It need not be concerned with the here and now, but can transport the participant to the past or future ... it can change the player from what he is to what he might be. It can make him examine his attitudes and those of others. It transforms the concept of learning because this learning takes place because it is necessary at that time, not as an end in itself to be stored away with the squirrel's nut against a future chill winter. (Tansey, 1971, p 4)

Tansey goes on to explain that simulation is a technique which simplifies reality, makes it accessible in a non-threatening way to classroom consideration and permits pupils to take decisions, the consequences of which can be worked through in a supportive environment. He claims:

... the teacher, as the representative of a system in which they (less able or uninterested pupils) have failed, is often viewed with hostility. His role in simulation changes ... he ceases to be a focal point ... learning becomes important and necessary to take part in the simulation and as a consequence the learning is effective. (p 6)

Simulation is used increasingly to pursue academic objectives (Walford, 1969; Carlson, 1969; Kirk, 1987), but the emphasis here is on problem-solving and value analysis, both key aspects of making decisions. The work of White and Lippitt (1968) indicated the effect on pupil behaviour of a democratic style of leadership. Their investigation suggested that such leadership produced initiative-taking ability and independent working capacity in adolescents. Similar findings appear in the more recent work of Abercrombie (1979). The coping skills identified in Chapter 1 (Figure 1.3) include 'move to independence' (14), and 'emotional autonomy' (15), and one can see the potential of simulation in that sphere.

Taylor and Walford (1974) made a succinct summary of the advantages of simulation exercises for secondary school pupils:

1. Players take on roles which are representative of the real world (cf Chapter 1, Figure 1.3, 'Major coping skills', 18) and then make decisions (cf Figure 1.3, 'Major coping skills', 5, 11, 14, 15) in response to their assessment of the setting in which they find themselves (cf Figure 1.3, 'Major coping skills', 4, 8, 9, 10, 16).
2. They experience simulated consequences which relate to their decisions and their general performance (cf Figure 1.3, 'Major coping skills', 15, 17, 18).
3. They monitor the results of their actions, and are brought to reflect upon the relationship between their own decisions and the resultant consequences (cf Figure 1.3, 'Major coping skills', 1, 7, 14, 15).

Thus simulation might be used in the guidance or tutorial period to pursue a wide range of socio-emotional objectives. It offers an atmosphere which is beneficial to self-esteem and a structure (democratic) which itself develops initiative-taking ability. The precise objectives to be pursued will obviously vary, but the underlying advantages outlined above are a consistent feature of the simulation exercise, and the children will be learning to make decisions.

Tansey (1971) pointed out that 'one of the greatest benefits of simulation is the ease with which particular simulations can be put together'. This is not to suggest that careful preparation is not needed, and that precise objectives need not be stated; it indicates rather the wide range of topics which can be approached via simulation.

What follows is an outline of a simulation I have used with 16-year-old students. It is offered as an easily prepared example of the technique, which is also inexpensive – no small consideration in the current economic climate.

AIM
To explore the attitudes and values that produce vandalising behaviour. To develop decision-making skills related to such behaviour.

SCENARIO
1. 15 minutes – A school has been burned to the ground; the 12-year-old who was responsible says, 'I was just bored.' A discussion takes place after the event between the following: the culprit, his friend who had refused to accompany him, his sister, his girlfriend, a policeman, his parents, his teacher, his headmaster, a neighbour.
2. 15 minutes – 300 milk bottles have been smashed and strewn over Newcastle United's pitch. There will be no home games for the rest of the season – the 12-year-old who was responsible says, 'I was just bored.' A discussion takes place after the event between the following: the culprit, his friend who had refused to accompany him, his sister, his girlfriend, a policeman, his parents, his teacher, his headmaster, a fan *or* (alternative)
3. On arriving at the local youth club at 8 pm a group of pupils find the disco equipment smashed and the television stolen. The 12-year-old finally caught says, 'I was just bored.' A discussion of the event takes place between the following: the culprit, the youth club leader, four members of the youth club, his parents.

DISCUSSION
30 minutes – The teacher will need to draw out attitudes to

selfishness	selflessness
destructiveness	constructiveness
adolescent view	adult view

Also suggestions from students on how to tackle the problem (if it is seen as a problem).

EVALUATION
The pupils involved in this exercise reacted with great spontaneity to the simulated situation. Initial embarrassment about role-playing was

rapidly overtaken by enthusiastic discussion of the 'real' problem, and the teacher involved was able to focus subsequent discussion of the exercise on the issue involved, pointing out how decisions had been made and might have been made.

The teacher must observe the action meticulously if he is to use the discussion to develop decision-making skills. He will note strongly expressed attitudes, inconsistencies, disagreements, and he must help the less verbal and the more tentative speakers to make their contribution.

By such methods, then, pupils can be helped to develop the confidence and skill to take initiatives and make decisions. If those skills are valued, practised and encouraged in school, both the decision-making described in the previous chapter as the culmination of counselling and the everyday decisions all our children must make will be that much easier to achieve.

It is the teacher's task, as group leader, to make the exercises developmental in the area of problem-solving ability and decision-making skill. He will do this by clarifying structures, helping to supply and analyse data, and by facilitating an evaluation of consequences. Data, logic and values are three indispensables in this area of teaching.

Data and decision-making

The availability of up-to-date information (seen by Moore [1970] as another key feature of effective guidance) becomes increasingly difficult as the pace of change increases. For example, the names on the map of Africa bear little relationship to the fact-laden geography most of us studied at O level, economic and work-related data changes weekly, and once stable positions and values fluctuate with bewildering rapidity. We can pretend a stability that does not exist, and indeed by default we sometimes do that. I recently picked up a book on banking as a profession, intended for 15-year-olds, which had been published in 1962. This pearl was buried in a school careers information library. Nevertheless, it would be entirely hypercritical to dwell on school inadequacies as collectors and purveyors of up-to-the-minute information, since teachers are in the same situation as everyone else in our society. We suffer from information overload. In the world of work (which our older pupils are about to enter) statistics, predictions, expansion and contraction occur and are reported daily. In education new modes of entry into technical and commercial careers supersede the old ones; new exams are suggested, piloted and adopted/rejected; teacher training now requires passes in GCSE maths and English; some engineers need a language, and so on.

Our society is in the middle of a data revolution. There is an enormous and exponentially increasing amount of information, and the means of access to it are changing rapidly. What our pupils need are 'search skills'. Since data accumulation is so vast, and since much of it rapidly loses validity, we all need methods of continually updating our information base. That base will clearly vary from one individual to another, but what will not vary is the certainty that it will change. Frequently a rich source of information is available, if only we know where to look. Our pupils need to know how to find and use library facilities, information services and the increasing number of computer-based data banks. Computer networking will undoubtedly expand the number, range and depth of their data sheets, and become increasingly accessible to more people. This is the world for which we are preparing our pupils, and any suggestion that information is a solid unchanging mass at which we nibble away in school is counterproductive.

In addition to the usual range of search skills that pupils are helped to display in most subjects (one still does find students coming up to university who are uncomfortable in a library), tutors, house staff, and pastoral specialists might develop exercises specifically designed to help pupils become more confident data searchers. For example, we could ask a group of 15-year-olds to work in groups of three to find out as much information as possible about the University of Newminster, giving them pointers on how such information might be collected. Children enjoy collecting and a mild competitive element adds spice to the game. They could be asked to collect data on local Youth Training Schemes, on self-help and co-operative work schemes, leisure possibilities, and so on. Again, the teacher will draw out the problems involved in searching, the social skills needed in approaching strangers, the reading skills and the recording skills required. The major point, of course, is that our pupils need to practise initiative-taking in seeking information. We fail them badly if we send them out into a data-rich world with search skills unpractised.

Logic and decision-making

Some years ago I discovered that a number of my pupils were exercising their decision-making skills by pushing envelopes containing dog dirt through the letter boxes of recently arrived Asian families. I made a very naïve response, trying to tackle it on the basis of the illogicality of the act. I even wrote the word 'ALL' in big letters on my board and each time someone used it to stereotype I put a red line through it. We talked about 'all Englishmen are snobs', 'all Italians love pasta', 'all Americans are brash', and I began to feel that my approach, through exposing faulty induction, was beginning to get somewhere. Then, quite without warning, someone made a crude racial comment; sticking to my logical tack, I asked the culprit, 'Danny, if I offered you £1000 to go on holiday anywhere you liked, with one condition – would you go?' A very positive response ensued with a discussion of where, doing what, and so on. 'The condition? Oh yes, I'd forgotten, Dan. You must either go with Ian Brady (at that time a recently convicted child murderer about whom my pupils had expressed strong views) or with one of the black doctors from the infirmary up the road.'

This was real school. No hiding behind Piagetian theory – think on your feet. I felt quite elated by the stunned silence. They were thinking about individuals, not stereotypes. Logic was winning. Then the crushing reply, 'Ah'd gan with the black doctor, but ah bet it'd smell better with the murderer.' What chance had logic when it was being subverted by layer after layer of deeply ingrained values. I recount the anecdote in some detail, in part because it illustrates so well the inadequacy of a merely cognitive approach. Yes, we need to look at reasons and rationalisations, but values are crucial. I also tell it because it highlights one area of decision-making that we have shied away from with great consistency – our response to pupils in a multi-cultural, multi-ethnic society.

Values and decision-making

Simon (1972) is one of several Americans who have been influential in developing educational responses to the area of value clarification and analysis (Simon and Clark, 1975; Rath and Simon 1978). He has identified three techniques which teachers tend to use in their attempts to achieve 'moral development' in their pupils. Traditionally they have engaged in an attempt to inculcate their values upon the young directly. It is usually a sincere, often subtle, attempt to reduce the pain of formulating personal values. This 'moralising' approach is increasingly less effective because of the several socialising agencies which compete for the attention of the young. The home can offer one code of values, the school another, the media a third, and the peer group a fourth (cf Reich and Adcock [1976], pp 47–8). Ultimately, the child must choose for himself, and the preparation offered in a moralising situation leaves him ill equipped to do so.

A second approach is to offer a *laissez-faire* attitude that says: no one value system can be viewed as right, so I will allow my pupils to forge their own values without deliberate interventions on my part. The difficulty here is that the young, left to their own devices, experience great confusion and conflict; they want intervention (cf Tibble [1964], pp 37–8) and help to make moral decisions.

The adult who tries to present himself as an attractive 'model' offers such help, but the young have many such models whose values often conflict. Who are they to follow? The current pop star, a footballer, a favourite brother or sister, an admired teacher at school? This third approach itself offers a kind of information overload. Heroes are important in adolescence, but simple imitation is impossible with so many different models.

Simon has developed a type of exercise which is designed to help young people sort out the inconsistencies. It uses the group effectively, relying on the strong influence adolescents have on each other. It does, however, require perceptive leadership if it is to achieve the goals outlined by Simon. They are that young people should be able:

1. To choose values freely, having considered many alternatives, and examined the consequences of the choice.
2. To be willing to prize and, in appropriate circumstances, publicly affirm those values.
3. Develop the ability to act consistently and in accord with the values established (p 19).

At the heart of the strategy is the evidence from group psychology that peer groups can help to initiate and support attitude change. Simon comments that, although this is a new technique and there is little empirical research on its effect as yet, his own findings suggest:

> that students who have been exposed to this approach have become less apathetic, less flighty, less conforming as well as less over-dissenting. They are more zestful and energetic, more critical in their thinking and more likely to follow through on decisions. (Simon, 1972, p 120)

A brief word on the role of the teachers involved in such an exercise is important. Of course, we are pursuing 'valuable' or 'productive' changes of attitude or behaviour, but there is a danger that moralising (even an attempt to indoctrinate) may occur in such a strategy. A democratic style of leadership will ensure that the leader, while recognising that his contribution will be very influential, must be involved in sharing his values with the group. The following example,

The Pennant Game, is an adaptation of a game which appears in Simon's book, but which has appeared in several similar works, and whose origins seem to lie in the mists of time. I have used it with great success and find that other teachers prize it too.

It is a source of continual amazement to teachers using the game for the first time how the most taciturn pupils become willing to share their values. An indication of how productive it is was given to me when a teacher described how he had asked a fifth year to fill it in as homework. 'How many do you think I got back from 78 pupils?' 'Thirty?' I replied tentatively. 'Eighty-two' was his triumphant reply. 'Four fourth years did it for fun.' Fun it is, but serious fun, for teachers can find in their pupils' fears, hopes, pride and personal mottoes, a rich vein of discussion, a source of illuminating debate, and great potential for developing decision-making skills about values. It is possible to vary the focus by asking pupils after discussion if they would like to change anything; the pennant remains a constant thread through all the discussions.

The use of these techniques in the classroom involves a degree of sharing initiatives with pupils that some teachers may not like. In that case, it is not for them. Other teachers may want to try but doubt that they have the skills to make it productive. That is certainly understandable, for few of us are trained to use such democratic classroom approaches. However, they do offer an invaluable means of skill development in pupils which no amount of teacher-focused approaches could achieve. Problem-solving, decision-making, value analysis and effective management of social situations can all be developed using this type of activity.

The game is used to help pupils identify and own their feelings and values – two elements of ourselves which powerfully influence our decisions. Two versions of the game appear in excellent books by Simon *et al.* (1972) and Brandes and Phillips (1978). The following is a slight variation on those themes, and further excellent suggestions can be found in Kirk's (1987) offering of experiential approaches to teaching and learning.

To the teacher. We are all adept at masking our feelings, often even from ourselves. The following game can reduce the stress of sharing feelings by apparently reducing the level of 'real' sharing. Precisely because the game is played in symbols the players share more easily than if we asked straight out 'What is your greatest fear?' Great care must be taken to protect vulnerable contributions, to value all participation. If aggression or cynicism surfaces, so much the better – they are easier to tackle out in the open than when carefully hidden.

PROCEDURE
1. Give each player a copy of Figure 7.1.
2. Instruct as follows:
    Your flag is divided into four parts. Imagine that you are designing a personal standard which will say something about you, as did the standards of the knights of old.
    In the top left square put a symbol of your greatest hope. Remember this is not a drawing test – stick men are fine, or you may wish to find something from the pile of magazines here to cut out and paste in.
    In the top right square symbolise your greatest fear in the same way. In the bottom left square put your greatest achievement, and in the bottom right square write a personal motto – something you feel you would like to live up to. (Give examples.)
3. You will find that pupils are very forthcoming in this exercise. When all the flags are complete, invite the pupils to speak about their pennants. Perhaps you could ask the whole class about each item, noticing shared and common fears and aspirations, and ask how they decided to make their choices.
4. Depending on the time available and the quality of the production, the pennants might all be displayed for the class.

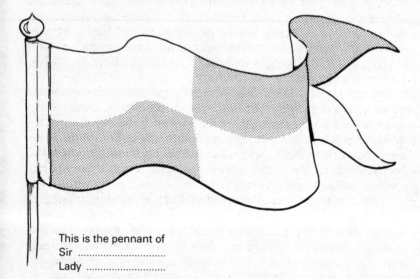

This is the pennant of
Sir ....
Lady ....

Figure 7.1. *The pennant game*

An atmosphere of trust is vital for this exercise to be successful. Most decision-making in schools involves consideration of issues that fall within the normal range of human difficulties. We are not confronted with life or death choices most of the time, merely time-consuming, significant selections of options which will make our life more pleasant or less pleasant, more productive or less so. Teachers make decisions about their teaching styles; children make decisions about subject choices; teachers make decisions about remedial work for this pupil, accelerated work for that pupil; children will make decisions about effort, commitment and attendance; staff make decisions about the range of sixth-form offerings; students decide whether or not to stay on at school after 16. Yet most of us, on reflection, will become aware of how frequently our decisions are made on the basis of whim or prejudice. We need to make a deliberate attempt to develop decision-making skills to reduce the accidental nature of so much of our choice-making. As in educational matters, so in personal development. 'The considered life' is not the monopoly of philosophers. This analysis of decision-making as a process, the use of value clarification and of simulation can be an effective way of helping our pupils to be more in control of their lives.

It is undoubtedly the case, however, that some difficulties will arise which may prove to be intractable. Some problem will face our children – and therefore ourselves as their teachers – to which we will not be able to see a solution. Despite long, conscientious efforts by teachers, a child may be seen to progress too little. In such circumstances, when the full competence of the school appears to have been fully stretched without achieving a solution to a problem, or an improvement in a difficult situation, a referral of a child to an agency or person outside the school may be appropriate. The problem does not have to be complex or serious; referral is appropriate when the problem to be solved requires expertise, knowledge or contact to be found outside the school. It is simply a way of offering the full resources of the community beyond the school to the child. A situation may arise when a referral is seen to be appropriate, but where it is impossible to find an agency which has personnel available to take on the referred child. Jones's (1975) finding that only 0.9 per cent of the children identified as maladjusted are treated by Child Guidance Units suggests that in order to cope with the rest of the maladjusted children, schools need to expand their repertoire of expertise. Nevertheless, teachers will have to make their decision to refer, and it is appropriate that we look at the question of referral here.

Referral

Shertzer and Stone (1971) point to the danger that teachers might become 'referral technicians', passing on to outside agencies problems they might well be able to tackle themselves. The likelihood of this happening is reduced simply because referral agencies are so over-burdened with cases. The ball is often left firmly in the school's court, and this is the reason why I have stressed so much the need for highly developed counselling skills in school. Whatever views we may hold about the teacher's role and the school's function, it is currently the case that many children in our schools will require skills from us in the area of counselling which most of us were never offered in our own training. Since referral is often not possible, we need those skills ourselves. The Summerfield Report (1968) on the Schools Psychological Service was quite unequivocal at this point:

> The British Psychological Society does not hold that no one but a psychologist should advise on signs of stress and the society would welcome a dissemination of appropriate psychological knowledge among teachers and others who might work as counsellors ... school counsellors and staffs of Child Guidance Units and the Schools Psychological Service should co-operate closely.

Clearly, the British Psychological Society feels that teachers could help them by avoiding premature referral. Increasingly, paraprofessionals are offering counselling support in medicine, social work and education, along the lines outlined by Hopson and Scally (1979) and Kanfer and Goldstein (1975).

That said, a school ought not to fall into the opposite trap, namely a feeling of omnicompetence and reluctance to pass on 'our children' to a different agency. When all the resources of the school have been fully deployed, with no sign of improvement in the child, the question of involving another agency must be raised. In 1959 a Working Party on the Social Services made the important point that:

> No one profession dealing with a range of human needs can make exclusive claims in relation to the others. Each has its essential function as well as its necessary overlap with others. (It will) ... enable a holistic approach to be made to the multiple needs of man.

Since that report, a constant theme in social service analyses of problems has been the need for close co-operation and sharing among the educational, medical and social services. Each group needs to place its professional skills at the service of its clients: the petty demarcation disputes which mark many of our relationships have led to more than one Maria Colwell. Too frequently, safeguards designed to protect the client have been used to protect the profession.

Intractable problem	Potential source of help
Poverty (clothes, food, equipment etc)	Social services
Suspected battered child	Social services, NSPCC, police, Childwatch
Educational subnormality, gifted child	Schools Psychological Service
Aggression, bullying, depression, timidity	Child Guidance Unit
Disruptive behaviour	Behavioural unit, LEA
Truancy	Educational welfare service
Teenage pregnancy, drug abuse, solvent abuse, alcohol abuse	School medical service, community health service, Child Guidance Unit
Delinquency	Police (not necessarily a formal contact)
Physical handicap	Social service, community health service
Jobs, unemployment	Careers service
Family difficulties	Local church, social services, Relate (formerly Marriage Guidance Council)
Illiteracy, innumeracy	Several voluntary organisations offer extra help
Cultural shock, cultural confusion	Local immigrant organisations, local religious leaders

Figure 7.2. *Problems and sources of help*

Schools might find it useful to compile a list like Figure 7.2, giving the name of a liaison officer in the outside agency and a telephone number. Clearly stated policies and procedures on referral should be made to all staff (cf the case study in Chapter 5). In addition, such a list raises the awareness of staff about liaising with outside agencies, and alerts them to the wide range of possible difficulties their pupils face. The areas of help identified are not exhaustive and clearly they will vary from one locality to another.

In Chapter 5, we considered the need to locate problems in school, and I suggested that one factor which reduced our inclination to look for problems below the surface was a feeling that we had neither the time nor the expertise to help in school – better let sleeping dogs lie.

Unfortunately, the dogs often awake at most inopportune moments and the foregoing list gives a brief indication of how many dogs there are. In that light, referral can be seen as an important part of the guidance services of any school.

PROCEDURES

It is all very well to say that we will need to refer pupils to the care of other agencies, but we need also to plan carefully how such referrals might take place. Schools will make specific plans on an individual basis that take into account the needs of their pupils and the available referral agencies in their area. Nevertheless, three basic areas need to be considered:

1. Identification of pupils needing referral.
2. The process by which referral is made (the child, the parents, the receiving agency).
3. Support, liaison and re-entry to school.

Identification

If a referral needs to be made in a crisis situation, the guidance system is beginning to creak. Ideally we should see the problem coming and referral should be the natural, planned culmination of a developing process. Chapters 4 and 5 looked at how we might extract needles from haystacks, and it is the use of that aspect of the school guidance system that is the key to effective referral. The issue is simple: What is the problem? Can the school cope? To answer the first part of the question, a case conference (cf Chapter 5) is invaluable. Again, if a representative from the probable receiving agency could attend the case conference, the process of the referral will be that much smoother. A detailed assembly of the data available should be used as an evidential base on which to make a decision about whether referral is appropriate or not. In answering the second part of the question, a high level of professional objectivity is needed. If feelings are running high (a serious incident has just occurred in school, a teacher has been abused), great care has to be taken that the response is not reactive. The purpose of the referral needs to be clearly stated, and the receiving agency has a right to know what is expected of it.

Occasionally a referral may be necessary in a crisis situation (eg in the event of a serious, potentially dangerous assault). Even in this case, a carefully prepared statement produced in an emergency case conference should be sent to the receiving agency at the earliest opportunity. All our pupils are our responsibility and we must be careful not to adopt a 'dustbin' approach to the most taxing of them.

These lines are being written at the time when the Elton Committee investigating school discipline is meeting. This is an area of concern to teachers, which involves the most skilled decision-making. What most of our critics fail to realise is that *control* is not the prime issue. In the final analysis we always have the means of *controlling* our pupils (see Figure 7.3). Our key task is to create the kind of environment in which learning can take place. When simply controlling pupils becomes the key issue, teachers really must (and indeed do) demand the right to refer and exclude pupils from school.

Physical restraint	Pharmacological restraint	Caning Beating	Verbal lashing Sarcasm	Logic Reason	Counselling
Straitjacket	Tranquillisers	Corporal punishment	Abuse		Relationships

Figure 7.3. *A control continuum*

All the methods mentioned in Figure 7.3 have been used in some circumstances, at some time. Few teachers would advocate the administration of tranquillising drugs, but they were used in educational establishments in the 1970s! If a pupil's behaviour is so outrageous that only strategies on the left-hand of the continuum will be effective in control, such a pupil needs to become the responsibility of a different kind of agency, not a school. Education is not about extrinsic control it is about self-control. That small number of pathological pupils who require control in order that other pupils might learn to be referred to specialist institutions (McGuiness and Craggs, 1986). Of course, not all referrals will involve problems of misbehaviour.

The referral process
Although most referrals will be remedial responses to some aspect of dysfunction in a child, it is possible to make a preventive referral or a developmental referral. For example, a child with grossly deficient social skills might be referred to a well-regarded youth club which has a constructive response to such referrals. A clear expectation of what will happen should be given to the youth leader who would also plan his work accordingly. Thus, in a safe, small group, social activities designed to help develop social skills could be planned.

More frequently, the referral will be remedial and, whatever the form, a child will always experience some level of rejection in being passed from one agency to another. With that feeling, there will be apprehension about the unknown, anxiety about being in the hands of a new person, and perhaps disappointment that a well-liked teacher has 'given up' on him. The school's personal contact with the child (probably head of house or year) must at all times show the unconditional positive regard for the child mentioned in the previous chapter. Reassurance and realism (the genuineness is identified by Truax and Carkhuff) will make it easier for the child to move productively into the hands of another helping agency.

When a referral is being discussed, it is crucial that parents be involved, unless the issue is one of child battering. Research suggests that parental attitudes are a prime influence on a child's progress at school, and for that practical reason alone – apart from the ethical consideration – they ought to be involved intimately in the education of their children. When referral becomes part of that education, consultation with parents must be an essential ingredient if it is to be successful. The honesty that should characterise the teacher's relationship with the child must clearly be equally present in the contact with the parent.

Support after referral
Responsibility for our pupils does not end when the referral is made. Indeed, liaison with the receiving agency is essential if a successful re-entry into the school is to be achieved. Unfortunately, it has been a regular experience of mine to see a referred child bloom in his new situation, only to wither away because his return to school was ill-planned, or worse, not planned at all. The process of communication between the referring and receiving agent must be two-way, the school assembling a detailed case study embodying all the factual up-to-date information mentioned in Chapter 4. This will be the basis on which the receiving agency will construct a strategy for helping the child. Equally, that agency must keep the school fully informed of procedures adopted, improvement seen, and difficulties encountered during the referral so that the child will be able, eventually, to return to his normal school. Nor should the school be in the least offended by a recommendation for further in-school treatment after the child's return. As teachers we are quite willing to accept the doctor's recommendation that a particular child ought not to do physical education for several weeks, but bristle with indignation if a psychiatrist suggests that the personality of a particular teacher has a destructive effect on a child, and that the two should be kept apart.

We can thus sum up the major features of referral:

1. It should occur when the child's difficulty needs the expertise of people not available in school, or responses not appropriate to a school (eg physical restraint).
2. It should be recommended in a reassuring, realistic way, involving both child and parents whenever possible.
3. The referral should always be accompanied by excellent communications between the school and the referral agency before, during, and after the referral.

Decision-making lies at the heart of our lives, and as the opening of this chapter suggested, the development of decision-making skills ought to lie at the heart of our educational efforts. Awareness of decision-making, analysis of the process and practice of it are essential ingredients in training children. Perhaps the final ingredient is teacher example, which might be analysed by asking ourselves, 'How many decisions did I let my pupils make at school today?'

Chapter 8

Accountability – The Need to Evaluate Our Guidance System

The issue of 'accountability' is being increasingly raised in educational discussions; limited resources, staffing cuts, and a constrained curriculum leave the hinted question 'how do you justify your salary?' hanging threateningly over us all. Politicians, parents and taxpayers no longer accept as dogma the bald view that 'education is good – so we must pay up'. Questions are asked about why the curriculum is devoted to different subjects, and whether or not the aims pursued are being achieved. Shaw (1973) asserted quite brutally in the USA that the future of guidance in secondary schools depended on its ability to show that it made a difference. The current government holds unequivocally to the competitive values of the market-place, echoing Shaw's view of a decade ago. Eraut (1981) provides a scholarly analysis of precisely *how* we might account – but account, we must.

Evaluation

Evaluation is a systematic attempt to show that some activity does make a difference, and that the difference relates to previously stated, valued aims. Educationalists are regularly exhorted to evaluate their progress, yet, for various reasons, little evaluatory activity occurs. There is almost a suggestion that the activity itself is valuable – that what teachers do is worthwhile, independent of the effects of what they do. Many reasons are given to explain the absence of accountability in education: evaluation takes up precious time better devoted to the real work of schools – teaching; the kinds of effects produced in education are not measurable; an assumption that all is well, a non-evaluatory prejudice in favour of what we are doing; perhaps a deep-seated worry that evaluation might expose real weaknesses we might not be able to eradicate. Whatever reasons led us to play down evaluation in the past, there are powerful, contrary motivations to reject them now. Pastoral care must, like the rest of the curriculum, be analysed with scrupulous care. As with other topics in the school curriculum, pastoral care must justify its position by showing that its effect is positive.

A recent conversation with a headteacher about guidance led him to ask:

> Is there any school which you think has a particularly good pastoral care system – one we might go and have a look at?

Several sprang to mind but I hesitated, feeling ill at ease with the idea that there existed some model of guidance which was transferable from school to school. I am convinced by Moore's (1970) assertion that there can be no ideal system of guidance and that constraints on different schools vary so greatly that to search for a model is pointless. Nevertheless, there is an increasing consensus among investigators that in effective pastoral systems certain areas are always well covered and that certain tasks are always well carried out. It is those areas and those tasks which must lie at the heart of any evaluation. Using the Moore (1970) survey, the systems analysis of Shaw (1973) and the descriptive analysis of HM Inspectorate (1979), McGuiness (1982) arrived at ten areas which would serve as useful focuses for an evaluation in any school. Figures 8.1 to 8.10 bring that analysis up to date.

Ten key issues

1. *Is the curriculum designed, constructed, implemented and monitored to ensure that the full range of potential for all pupils is being met?*
Specific areas to be examined will include the following:

   a) The degree of integration between the academic and pastoral specialists in the planning and operation of the curriculum.
   b) The school's examinations policy. Does the school bear in mind the impact on all its pupils of examinations? What of projects for GCSE where some children benefit from strong home support in the form of books available and parental involvement? Can school supplement the absence of such resources for some pupils?
   c) The methods used to indicate to the school community that we prize all pupils regardless of academic skill. This will involve looking at how awards are given; what hidden curriculum statements are made; whether prizes are won consistently by children from one group in the school.
   d) Provision for our most able children and for our least able. Is

| Focus | Criteria for evaluation | | | |
	Operational data	Subjective data	Outcome data	Evaluatory comment
1. Degree of integration between pastoral and academic groups	Termly meeting of both groups. Case conferences occur regularly	Staff questionnaire: pastoral staff feel there is insufficient consultation	Several academic decisions made in case consultation with pastoral staff. But many low-ability pupils under-participating	Need to sort out pastoral staff's reservations. Need to look at needs of academically less able children
2. School exam policy	Numbers of pupils doing GCSE and A level	Pupil survey, staff survey, parent survey	Preparation of pupils passing different exams	Appears to be a realistic entry policy for exams – but note item above on needs of academically less able
3. Hidden curriculum	No analysis regularly undertaken	Pupil survey, parent survey, staff survey. 'What does this school prize?' 'What does this school value?'	Identify examples of statements about school values – cups awarded (for what), status given etc	Do we have a tendency to under-value less able children? Or do we so concentrate on less able that able children are neglected?
4. Teaching methods	Not discussed. Seen as private	Pupil survey, staff survey		Do we need to plan pupil exposure to a variety of methods?
5. Grouping	Identify types of groups used	Pupil survey, staff survey	Identify social, emotional and academic effects – with evidence	Is early mixed ability approach abandoned too quickly?

Figure 8.1. *An evaluative procedure for pastoral care – Topic: Curriculum*

| | Criteria for evaluation | | | |
Focus	Operational data	Subjective data	Outcome data	Evaluatory comment
1. How is data collected?	Identify formal, informal sources regularly used	Staff survey on efficiency of data collection	Is adequate data available?	Is there a tendency to overlook children who are quiet (depressives, isolates)?
2. Case conference	How often do they occur? Who is there?	Staff survey. Outside agency comments	How many 'plans for action' have emerged from case conferences?	Are case conferences simply informal staffroom chats? Are outside agencies excluded?
3. Parental/outside agency involvement	Number of parental visits. Type of contacts. Same with outside agency	Parental survey, staff survey, survey of outside agency	To what extent (evidence) have parents/outside agencies contributed to individualising pupils?	How can we break down staff resistance to parental/social service collaboration?
4. Form tutors	Precisely what do the tutors do? When is data collected? How?	Pupil survey – do they see themselves as *known*? Staff survey – do they *know* each of their pupils?	Collect examples of efficient individualising. What slip-ups have occurred?	Are some pupils slipping from view because of limited tutor commitment? Response?

Figure 8.2. *An evaluative procedure for pastoral care – Topic: Individualising pupils*

145

| Focus | Criteria for evaluation | | | |
	Operational data	Subjective data	Outcome data	Evaluatory comment
1. Record system	Is there one on each child? Is it factual? Regularly reviewed and revised?	Are staff satisfied with content? Method of review?	Check records of consultations. How many?	Do all tutors carry out a thorough review of their form's records?
2. Storage of records	Are they secure, yet available for professional consultation?	Are staff happy with access level? Are they professional with data received?	Check records of consultations made by staff – by whom? Down to what level of staff?	Are we happy that no one below assistant head of year is consulting records? Do outside agencies help sufficiently with records? Do parents have access?
3. Responsibility for records	Who fills in record card? Who reviews it? How often is there a statement of school policy?	Are staff happy with system?	Are record entries dated and initialled? Is there evidence of regular review?	Is the responsibility too *ad hoc*? Do we need to establish clear responsibilities for specific tasks?
4. Children at risk	Is there provision for data to be collected on children at risk?	How satisfied are the social services with this arrangement?	Do we consult regularly and early with colleagues in social services?	How can liaison with social services be improved?

Figure 8.3. *An evaluative procedure for pastoral care – Topic: Records in school*

Criteria for evaluation

Focus	Operational data	Subjective data	Outcome data	Evaluatory comment
1. Recording staff attitudes. Arriving at a working consensus	How much in-service in this area occurs? Levels of attendance?	Survey academic staff. Survey pastoral staff	What participation in pastoral activity occurs?	Can negative attitudes in 25% of staff (cf survey) be changed? If not, how can pastoral system cope?
2. Involvement in pastoral work	How many uncommitted staff have a pastoral responsibility?	Staff survey	Is there varied input from pastoral staff (time, enthusiasm)?	Do we need to use only the fully committed in pastoral care?
3. Headteacher attitudes	What statements on policy exist? Does he attend committees, work on pastoral care?	Staff survey	How are resources allocated to pastoral care? Timetable, money, staff, leave of absence for courses	How can we cope with the community pressure on head to use resources on prestigious projects for only a few children?
4. Pupil views	How many pupil-initiated contacts occur?	How do pupils see staff attitudes to them?		

Figure 8.4. *An evaluative procedure for pastoral care – Topic: Staff attitudes to pastoral care*

Focus	Criteria for evaluation			
	Operational data	Subjective data	Outcome data	Evaluatory comment
1. Trained personnel	Is there a trained counsellor on the staff? Do staff have counselling skills? Is in-service work used to develop skills? How often?	Pupil survey – would they use staff as a resource if problems arose? Staff survey – do they feel they need counselling expertise (personality?) available to them as a referral possibility?	Evidence of one-to-one work with pupils? Any group counselling approaches? Are there pupils who drift from year to year without any productive school intervention?	Is it appropriate to explore what use might be made of a trained counsellor? Who in staff might be supported for training? Do we need to become more aware of the use of counselling?
2. Paraprofessional skills	Is there liaison with a counsellor-training group? Are house heads and other pastoral staff aware of the nature of counselling skill? Have they attended basic courses? How many?	Pupil survey – as above. Staff survey – as above. Seek comments from objective, skilled outside consultant. (Local university, polytechnic etc)		What in-school staff development in this area is appropriate? What should school policy be?

Figure 8.5. *An evaluative procedure for pastoral care – Topic: Availability of counselling*

Criteria for evaluation

Focus	Operational data	Subjective data	Outcome data	Evaluatory comment
1. School ethos	List areas of direct pupil participation in decision making. What responsible posts do pupils have? Are all staff involved in decision making?	Pupil survey – do they feel responsible? Staff survey – do they feel pupils are sufficiently – too much involved?	Evidence of involvement in school? Vandalism of property in school? Level of attendance at meetings?	Do members of the school community see it as a community where all are responsible? If not, what can be done to change the perception?
2. Classroom ethos	How many teachers regularly use participatory pedagogical approaches?	Pupil survey – do they see their learning as active or passive?	When decisions are made, are they sound in terms of effectiveness? (Look at frequent subject changes etc)	How often are our pupils called on to make a decision in school – or participate in one?
3. Information	Is there a resource centre or careers FE, HE? Is it regularly brought up to date?	Pupil survey – where do they seek information? How do they view the resource centre?	Can pupils seek, use data effectively in simulated and real decision making?	How might one ensure better data availability?

Figure 8.6. *An evaluative procedure for pastoral care – Topic: Decision-making skill*

	Criteria for evaluation			
Focus	Operational data	Subjective data	Outcome data	Evaluatory comment
1. Role description	Is there a list of responsibilities for each member of the team?	Staff survey – do they feel a blurring of areas of responsibility?	Have problems got lost because no one was clearly responsible?	Do we need to write, revise a list of responsibilities (eg on records, truants, ill children, discipline matters)?
2. Communication lines	Is there a clear statement of procedures (a) normally (b) in emergencies?	Staff survey – do they know where to turn for help? At what point help should be sought?	Has a problem got lost in the pipeline? Is there evidence that communication flows smoothly in both directions?	Is the staff noticeboard used effectively – are all used to viewing it as an emergency contact line?
3. Form teacher	How many volunteers? By whom and on what topics are form tutors consulted? Is consultation formal or informal?	Staff survey – analyse skill interests, perceptions of form tutorial role. Pupil survey – do they know their form tutor? Feel trust towards him?	What contacts between form tutor and their pupils occur?	All surveys suggest this 'point of first contact' is crucial. Needs to be analysed meticulously

Figure 8.7. *An evaluative procedure for pastoral care – Topic: Distribution of responsibilities*

| | Criteria for evaluation | | | |
Focus	Operational data	Subjective data	Outcome data	Evaluatory comment
1. Is there a period on the timetable specifically for pastoral purposes?	How much time? How is it distributed? When does it occur?	Staff survey – is it useful, used appropriately? Pupil survey – is it useful, used appropriately?	Measures of pupil change at end of syllabus, eg sociogram, self-esteem analysis	Are we checking the use teachers make of this period with sufficient care?
2. Do we have a full written syllabus for pastoral care time?	For how many years?	Staff survey. Pupil survey	To what extent are syllabus objectives met?	Can we improve the coherence of our pastoral syllabus?
3. What level of integration of this syllabus with other areas of the curriculum occurs?	With RE (values), English (communication), maths (budgeting), geography (career choice), history (social awareness), drama (social skills)	Staff survey – is integration sufficiently planned? Too *ad hoc*? Pupil survey – do they perceive any links in teaching?	Any team teaching? Any commonly constructed syllabus? Any joint projects?	Pastoral period is out on a limb, despite the possibility of collaboration with colleagues. Could a change here be productive?
4. Accountability	Is the tutorial period checked as rigorously as the rest of the curriculum?	Staff survey	What formal evaluatory comments have been made in the past two years?	Do we need to put this period under the evaluatory microscope? What is it for? Are we achieving aims?

Figure 8.8. *An evaluative procedure for pastoral care – Topic: Tutorial time*

	Criteria for evaluation			
Focus	Operational data	Subjective data	Outcome data	Evaluatory comment
1. What referral possibilities exist for the school?	Do we have an easily accessible list? Phone numbers? Contact person?	Staff survey	What referrals have been made? With what kind of difficulties?	Do we need to publicise available referral services more? Are we too eager to refer difficult cases?
2. Liaison before, during and after referral	What contacts are made with a receiving agency during the referral process?	Staff survey, outside agency survey	Identify by case study several referral processes which have occurred in school	Do referred children slip out of our view? Are all concerned with the child in school kept informed of progress?
3. Involvement of outside agents	How many visit school? For what purpose? Whom do they see?	Staff survey, outside agency survey	Identify results of liaison with social workers, EWOS etc – or results of failure to liaise	Is prejudice, ignorance, fear, lack of respect between education and social services working to the detriment of pupils in need?
4. Follow-up and re-entry	How many visits do we make to the referral agency to check our pupils' progress?	Staff survey, outside agency survey	What success do we have with pupil re-entry after referral?	Do we tend to see referral as the end of the affair – accepting the child back without having followed his progress carefully?

Figure 8.9. *An evaluative procedure for pastoral care – Topic: Outside agencies*

152

| | Criteria for evaluation | | | |
Focus	Operational data	Subjective data	Outcome data	Evaluatory comment
1. Contact with parents	How many parents respond to initial contact?	Parent survey, staff survey	What productive data, help is received via this contact?	Can we improve contact methods? How can we contact non-responders?
2. How is contact, once established, maintained?	Do we have PTA? Open-door policy? Parental visiting day etc?	Parent survey, staff survey	What percentage of parents continue to visit, have interest in school?	How can parental involvement be improved?
3. School and the community	Do we present ourselves to the local community in plays, sport, community service etc?	Parent survey, staff survey	What plays, sport, visits have been undertaken?	Can we make school less uninviting to the local community? A source of pride for it? Can the community help us?
4. Children of parents with low interest in school	Do we have homework rooms? Do we have particular help strategies?	Pupil survey (great care in construction of this), staff survey	Are pupils whose parents 'never come' fully supported by the school?	Parents' attitudes are crucial to educational success – but school can mitigate disadvantage. Are we doing enough?

Figure 8.10. *An evaluative procedure for pastoral care – Topic: Parents*

either group not fully stretched, offered appropriate teaching?

e) Teaching methods – they speak loudly to our pupils about their value, our relationship with them, our view of knowledge and learning. What do they say? Do we monitor them systematically?

f) Educational guidance – on what basis do our pupils make option choices? What help are they given? What are the results of the choices in terms of personal satisfaction, needs for later change, appropriateness for pupil's further or higher education aspirations or career prospects?

g) School grouping policy – what led us to adopt streaming, setting, banding or mixed ability grouping. Are our expectations being realised? What are the academic, social and individual effects of our approach?

2. *Is every pupil in the school known? Are they individualised on the basis of sound, up-to-date, factual information?*
Specific areas to be examined will include the following:

a) How is data on pupils assembled, disseminated, checked and stored?

b) Precisely what informal and what formal data collection is undertaken? Are pupils themselves involved?

c) Is there a case conference facility to discuss children with chronic and/or complex problems?

d) Are parents and outside agencies asked to help in assembling an appropriate database for educational decision-making?

e) Do form tutors have a specific responsibility in data collection on their 30 pupils? What is that responsibility?

f) Is there evidence of failure in the data collection, eg a sudden, unforeseen crisis for a child, an undetected difficulty? How did this slip through the net? Can the system be improved?

3. *Is the record system of the school assembled on the basis of evidence, not opinion? Is it systematically reviewed and is access open to all who are concerned with the education of the children? Are the pupils involved via Records of Personal Achievement? Profiles?*
Specific areas to be examined will include the following:

a) Does the school have a record on each pupil which is factual, full, systematically kept up to date?

b) Are the records reviewed on an annual basis, each form tutor accepting responsibility for the records of the 30 children in his form?

c) Are records kept securely but available for professional consultation by all members of staff and appropriate outside agencies?

d) Are staff fully aware (written instructions) of their responsibilities *vis-à-vis* records?

e) How professional is the staff with confidential information? What failures have occurred? How can standards be maintained?

f) Are all entries on the record card dated and signed?

g) Has a serious discussion of parental rights of access to record cards taken place?

h) Is there provision for a 'Children at Risk' file? Has the Social Services Department been consulted?

4. *Are staff attitudes towards pastoral care positive?*
Specific areas to be considered will include the following:

a) Are all staff given an opportunity to say clearly what their attitude to this area of the curriculum is? (In-service day, curriculum workshop, questionnaires)

b) Does this system have teachers with negative attitudes towards pastoral care as part of its personnel? Can they be used positively? (eg Dissenters as refiners of practice.)

c) What evidence (allocation of resources, recruitment of staff, timetabling etc) is there of the headteacher's attitude to pastoral care?

d) What proportion of staff have any training in the various skills of pastoral care? What possibility of in-service training is available/made use of?

e) How do pupils view the pastoral system? What do they see to be the attitude of the staff?

5. *Is counselling expertise available for those in the school who need and want it?*
Specific areas to be considered will include the following:

a) Is there a trained counsellor on the staff?

b) Have any staff members attended courses designed to develop paraprofessional counselling skills?

c) What counselling expertise is available for referral outside the school?

d) Has the school crystallised a clear policy on counselling? Where is this policy stated?

6. *Does decision-making skill appear as a skill objective in curriculum planning? Is appropriate information available as a basis for sound decision-making?*

Specific areas to be considered will include the following:

a) What aspects of school organisation allow pupils to participate in decision-making?
b) What techniques/strategies are used in classrooms to develop skills in problem-solving, decision-making, values selection?
c) Do teaching methods encourage initiative and independence in the pupils or do they promote passive, accepting attitudes?
d) In preparation for adult life, is there a well-supplied resource centre with up-to-date information on jobs, further and higher education opportunities and leisure possibilities?

7. *Is there a clear definition of areas of responsibility in the school, a clear statement of roles?*

Specific areas to be considered will include the following:

a) Is there a list of specific tasks allotted to each member of the pastoral care team?
b) What is the line of communication in the pastoral system? How is this communication carried out – formally or informally?
c) What specific responsibilities do individuals have for truancy, referral, record-keeping and integrating the academic and pastoral systems? How is it checked that these responsibilities are carried out?
d) Is the vital role of the form teacher as 'contact adult' recognised by including that teacher in all decision-making on the children in his care?

8. *Does the school have a timetabled tutorial/pastoral period?*

Specific areas to be considered will include the following:

a) Is there a syllabus of areas to be covered during a regular pastoral period?
b) Does that syllabus include skills and attitudes among its objectives?
c) Is the pastoral time integrated with teaching in other parts of the curriculum (RE and values, English and communication, maths and budgeting, geography and careers choice, history and social awareness, drama and social skills)?

d) Is the tutorial period evaluated with the same vigour as other parts of the curriculum? What criteria are used to judge its success?

9. *Does the school have clear communication lines with appropriate outside agencies? Can it be claimed that there is a mutual respect between school and local outside agencies?*
Specific areas to be considered will include the following:

a) Does the school possess a list of locally available referral agencies, with a telephone number and a contact person?
b) Is this list available to all staff whose responsibility it is to make external referrals?
c) Are staff, whose task it is to make internal referrals, kept informed of and involved with a referral outside the school?
d) Are representatives of outside agencies invited to consult and contribute to records when appropriate?
e) Are representatives of outside agencies invited to case conferences when appropriate?
f) Are all referrals followed up, and is there a clearly planned 're-entry' procedure for pupils who are to return to school?

10. *What percentage of the parent body is involved in the school's work? Is the performance of the new governing body being carefully monitored?*
Specific areas to be considered will include the following:

a) Are all parents contacted at the beginning of a child's school career? What follow-up occurs if the contact is ignored?
b) Is the initial contact maintained throughout the school career of the child?
c) On what occasions are parents invited to school? Is there an open-door policy? PTA? Exhibition day? Parental visits day?
d) Does the school go into the wider community? On community service, performing arts, music, plays, sport?
e) Are parents invited into school to meet staff socially?
f) What policy exists to help children whose parents give clear evidence that they do not value school very much?

All the foregoing topics will merit attention, but the important element will not be the question – or even the answer. The meat of the evaluation is the *evidence* for the answer. It is possible to select one particular area for analysis, say, record cards or parental involvement, or to undertake an evaluation of the whole pastoral programme. If it is decided that the latter course is appropriate, different teachers can be given responsibility for different topics.

Data collection sheets

The figures suggest a way in which information might be accumulated. After a topic has been identified (records, parental involvement, guidance and the curriculum, role distribution etc) different focuses can be analysed in detail for three types of evidence.

1. *Operational data*
   On an operational level, what have the guidance staff done? Enumerate meetings with parents, record card reviews, meetings with pastoral staff, and so on. This looks at pastoral activity.
2. *Subjective data*
   By asking pupils, colleagues, parents and representatives of outside agencies to fill in questionnaires or give written submissions to the evaluatory committee, a clear pattern of perceptions in different groups can be observed. This looks at reactions to pastoral activity.
3. *Outcome data*
   What behavioural evidence is there in terms of pupil performance that guidance is producing effects? Evaluation presupposes the existence of objectives which are open to evaluation. The broad aims and specific objectives underlying evaluation must be carefully identified by each school.

These procedures are examples of a possible approach. They need to be specifically constructed by each school to meet its own needs. If 3. is unsatisfactory, you may find the reason why in 1. and 2.

It cannot be over-emphasised that evidence is the key to evaluation. Although it is possible for an outsider to identify areas that ought to be scrutinised, the precise question to be asked and evidence to be collected will need to be worked out school by school. The foregoing figures offer brief examples of the types of data which might be gathered.

Setting aside for a moment the data accumulation aspect of evaluation, anyone who has been involved in, for example, a general inspection, will recall how coming under scrutiny focuses the mind. Thus evaluation can be a 'consciousness-raising' exercise. All involved in it begin to sharpen perceptions, improve critical skills and develop creative responses to problems. The improvements which often emerge as a result of that will invariably compensate for the effort involved in the evaluatory exercise.

Summary

Evaluation must be undertaken if pastoral care is to merit the status it has been accorded in recent educational surveys.

Aims, refined into specific objectives, need to be discussed from the point of view of *value* and *feasibility*.

Evidence must be collected on the *operation* and *outcomes* of pastoral work in the school.

Subjective views of staff, pupils, parents and outside collaborators will shed light on our successes and failures, offering useful diagnostic insights, particularly on the latter.

Evaluation will result in the identification of areas of strength (to be built on) and areas of weakness (to be remedied). A 'Plan of Action' is the final phase of the evaluation. This may take the form of a series of specific recommendations which will be analysed in the next evaluation.

Chapter 9

No Opting Out!

> It is clear that we have no experts in this sort of urban education anywhere. The most expert are those professionals who are there every day, engaging in the fray. But they are reaching out and it is for this reason (not because the universities have any answers) that some kind of liaison is critical. (Silberman, 1970, p 450, quoting from Cunningham)

This must be the spirit in which this chapter is written. Silberman, just before making the realistic statement above, had given an amusing and salutary account of the attempt of an American university department of education to take responsibility for one term in a New York high school. After careful thought and meticulous planning the department began the brave experiment. After less than a week, the dean writes his rueful conclusion:

> We got the hell kicked out of us ... our staff has been through a shattering experience.

No one who has ever worked in an urban secondary school can ever belittle the herculean efforts that are made in them. Indeed, a recent report by the International Labour Organisation on teaching and stress (1981) identifies the toll; they reported that 25 per cent of teachers in Britain suffered from stress affecting their health, a condition called 'burnout' by the Americans and linked to battle fatigue. Dunham (1984) is one of several authors who try to respond to the profession's needs in this area. This is the reality of the classroom, and the context within which I must frame my closing comments.

The nineteenth-century legacy

We seem to be caught in a trap set in the nineteenth century. Our schools were organised then to cope with a set of problems and socialisation issues that grew out of the nineteenth century, and since then we have tinkered with the machine trying vainly to use this outmoded, almost obsolete, contraption to face problems it was never designed to meet, problems which could not, in its earliest years, have been foreseen.

It is not a gross over-simplification to say that in 1870 the nation's new, free education service reflected two major concerns of its planners: (a) that it should help to supply a basically educated workforce for the then current industrial expansion, and (b) that it should ensure that this newly literate working class would not use its new skills for mischief. In short, schools should prepare pupils for work without unduly awakening political or social aspirations. Andrew Bell put it succinctly at the beginning of the nineteenth century:

> There is a risk of elevation, by an indiscriminate education, of the minds of those doomed to the drudgery of daily labour, above their condition, and thereby render them discontented in their lot. (Bell, 1805)

Revolutions had recently occurred in France, Germany and Italy, and even by 1860 there were rumblings in Russia. Discussion in and out of Parliament reflected the fear that damage to the social fabric might be done by universal free education. That early historical context continues to have its influence today; our schools are still largely influenced by those two focuses – work and obedience. Part of our problems as educators comes from the radical change of context within which schools operate (see Figure 9.1).

There is now a vast subculture of young people in our large cities who have never worked and, although Government figures suggest that unemployment figures are being held (and even reduced), what they fail to point out is the altered structure of the labour market. The jobs which disappeared during the 1970s were relatively well-paid, pensioned, health and safety protected. The new jobs tend to be part-time, ill-paid, non-pensioned and with reduced statutory protection. This may be an inevitable transitional characteristic of a post-industrial society but it does radically alter the traditional motivational aspect of hundreds of thousands of young people in school. The work ethic and economic need must be reviewed before we continue to use them as motivators of pupils in school. A recent study carried out on behalf of the Spanish government (with currently the most buoyant economy in Europe) estimates that they will need 100 years to offer a reasonable chance of work to all their youngsters.

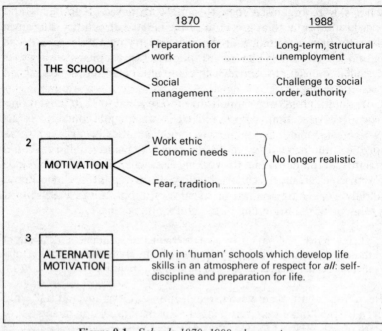

Figure 9.1. *Schools 1870–1988: changes in context*

Realities of the twentieth century

Piven and Cloward (1972) shed light on the other aspect of the school's activity. They show how periodically from the early Middle Ages great peaks of unemployment have led to social dislocation and public disorder. Authority is challenged, the social order and its organisational representatives which include schools are seen as unjust, oppressive and protective of privilege. Fear and tradition no longer serve to deter radical questioning of fundamentals. Thus, work and obedience are no longer the binding force they were in school, and Waller's (1932) description of the school as 'a despotism in a perilous state of equilibrium' indicates why we are finding schools increasingly difficult to manage – the equilibrium is being lost. How do we motivate when there is no carrot (work prospects) and no stick (fear of the teacher)? This uncompromising question is posed most eloquently by dissident pupils and over-worked teachers – it appears in a more scholarly fashion in Coffield's (Coffield *et al.*, 1986) impressive 'Growing Up at the Margins' – but it is a theme which has been constantly presented during the last decade (McGuiness and Craggs,

1986; Hemmings, 1980; McMullen, 1978; Patterson, 1974).

In the 1970s we have had to face the reality of secondary education for all up to the age of 16. Schools now have to work not just with children but with young men and women, not just the gifted but with the whole range of ability. Yet our curriculum methods were designed for able children. It is little wonder that the less able young adult rejects it. The DES (1981) exhortation that '*what* is taught in school and *the way* it is taught should help *all* children to realise their potential to the fullest extent' must become more than a pious hope. It needs to be planned for by the teaching profession. It has become of crucial importance that the vast effort and expertise expended and developed by the profession should not be eroded by a retrograde implementation of the National Curriculum, which fails totally to recognise the success of the last 15 years.

Hopson and Scally (1981) outline with challenging clarity the world of the 1980s and 1990s. Not only is our clientele radically different but we are now being called on to prepare that clientele for a world which is changing at full speed, almost beyond recognition. One of the main features of that world will almost certainly be a vast amount of structural unemployment. Watts (1978) asked fundamental questions about a school curriculum based on the work ethic. What value has it when increasingly there is going to be less work? A recent collation of figures by the Teesside Industrial Mission (1980, unpublished) indicates that by the year 2000, Asia will need 370 million new jobs, black Africa 160 million, Latin America 130 million, and western nations 150 million. These figures and their inexorable direction are chillingly echoed in Merritt's *World Out of Work* (1982). This will be occurring at a time when fewer humans will be needed as less costly and more efficient machines take over routine, dangerous and boring work. In April 1981, Olivetti announced that much of their European operation was to be transferred to Third World countries since production costs – and labour costs – are so much lower there. We will see work opportunities drift from high-wage economies (our own) to low-wage economies (the Third World) and a move to increase productivity by using machines instead of men. Viewed against this background, the warning in Hopson and Scally's work cannot be ignored. Indeed, the House of Commons Select Committee on Unemployment explains the mechanism quite clearly. A major cost in manufacture and service is labour cost, thus shedding labour (made possible by new technology) increases profit. Thus managers have a responsibility to shareholders to shed jobs.

We have arrived at the theorist's dilemma. While analysis of the problem can be as radical as one wishes, response to that analysis is constrained by economics, resources and people. It is inevitably a slow response. By the time the profession had adjusted to the 1960s, with comprehensive schools and ROSLA, it found itself in the 1980s. Whatever happened to the 1970s? Do we have any room for manoeuvre?

The beginning of an answer, I suggest, lies in looking carefully at the nature in schools. It is not the rapidity of change that hurts but the lack of consensus – the adversarial nature of it. Revolution involves crushing opposition and brooking no criticism. We need to develop a system in schools for managing change that facilitates consensus and encourages a contribution to the change from all concerned. This may seem a forlorn hope as we look objectively at our nineteenth-century machine chugging dutifully but inimaginatively towards the twenty-first century. We need to look at the educational issues, not at timetables, money or staffing – important though they are. If we can formulate and arrive at a degree of consensus about the direction of education in 'our schools', then change will be possible. National considerations, like examinations, jobs, further and higher education entrance requirements, will remain constraints on our thinking, but 'our school' needs to direct its mind to analysing the curriculum for 'our pupils'. This must involve all our staff if we are not to continue the divisive and counter-productive approach of the academic versus the pastoral specialist teacher.

> Most schools have found it necessary to set up a pastoral network, but only when all staff feel involved is the academic work effectively supported by this network. No pastoral system can function satisfactorily divorced from the working life of the school. (*Curriculum 11–16*, 1977)

More recently, the Inspectorate has commented: 'All teachers are involved in the personal and social development of pupils. It is something they cannot opt out of because it is intrinsic to the nature of education itself.' (DES, 1987)

This positive statement by the Inspectorate can be turned over to present a more provocative face: 'If all staff are not involved in the pastoral network, we cannot expect the academic work of the school to be effective.' A further logical extension completes the equation; that there are, in fact, very few schools in which *all* staff can be said to be involved in pastoral work, so the fact that large numbers of our pupils seem to derive little benefit from school is to be expected until that lack of involvement changes.

We arrive back at our point of departure – there can be no opting out. The personal development of our pupils is, as the Inspectorate points out (and the current Home Secretary recently agreed), the central purpose of education. Hemmings' (1980) challenge that we should not engage in 'the Betrayal of Youth' is one we must answer.

Pupil needs – some case studies

The following cases, with some suggested issues for examination, might be used by a school staff to explore the simple question, 'What do our children need to equip them for their lives as adults?'

CASE ONE
Clive (represents the top 20 per cent of our children – those who go on to do degree courses). No one case can adequately represent the wide range of young people in their group properly. Clive is not atypical.

I'm in my second year of university, reading French. I was very successful in my first-year examinations and my tutor tells me I ought to get a first if I work hard. I do play soccer for the university and training does eat into my study time. I have an academic tutor mouthing nostrums like 'Firsts are for the single-minded' and my moral tutor telling me that the social aspect of university life is as important as the academic. I'd like to get a first, maybe do research for a bit, or apply to the civil service. I've never really given much thought to work. It always seemed so far away but, in one year, I'll have to start making decisions.

At least with a first in French I'm not sure to join the great unwashed. I suppose that is one advantage of having some brains. I feel desperately sorry for the unemployed – I suppose they must pay the inevitable price for lack of talent or application.

Do I resent welfare benefits? Why should I? I have a grant, so why shouldn't they have some state support too? What I do resent are the vast redundancy payments in the public sector and the protected status of civil servants, teachers and the like. We should all be exposed to market forces – artificial protection of public sector groups disturbs the economy. If a university hasn't enough students, chop the staff. Let's all be treated the same. If no one wants to buy our wares then we must join the unemployed.

I have thought about teaching as an easy option – an extra year on a grant – and I understand there is still a shortage of French teachers. I do feel a bit guilty at the thought of school-university-school as a way through life, but maybe that's the easiest way.

I've no idea if I've the temperament for teaching – or for the civil service for that matter. I do know that industry would appal me – all that noise, dirt and pollution.

In school terms Clive is a success. Seeing him two years on might make us think more carefully about that accolade. Perhaps we can ask the following questions about him:

- What might teachers have done to help Clive cope with his immediate and future situation?
- Knowing his current situation, what needs has he that school might have tried to supply (knowledge, attitudes, skills)?
- Would you feel happy about Clive's social development?
- Do you regard his attitude to industry as one which might be developed in your school?
- What is his attitude to education and learning?
- How are you helping the Clives in your school now?
- Do you regard your job as well done if you help him to three good A levels?

CASE TWO

Fiona, and her friend on the Youth Training Scheme, represent the next 30 per cent of the ability range. In that group the least able performer will be producing work at the level of the former Grade 4 CSE – the norm for the average 16-year-old. At the top end of the range, pupils will be getting the equivalent of four or five GCSEs; a few years ago they would have taken apprenticeships, gone into nursing, teaching, banking, and so on. Increasingly higher qualifications are sought as competition for the small number of jobs becomes fiercer.

Well – I usually get up with my mam – she teaches at a primary school near our house, so we're up about eight. My dad used to get up with us at the same time, but he lies in sometimes now. He used to work in a college of education, but it got closed and he was made redundant. I think he got some money for that, but we don't seem to have as much as we used to when they both worked. They're different now – more moody and irritable – less interested in us. Oh, yes – there's Brian, my brother, he's 20 and works for Abbey Life. He's got a newer car than my dad. I think dad feels badly about how well Brian's doing.

I left school 18 months ago – just before my dad was made redundant. I wasn't too good at school; anyway, look where exams got him – on the scrap heap at 44. I tried – my mam and dad spent hours helping me. I got one O level, in RE. Brian said if I'd done woodwork as well I could get an apprenticeship with an undertaker – ha! ha! I was so useless at school work I couldn't face going back to try again. I persuaded my mam and dad to let me leave and look for a job. My head of house showed me my reference – very complimentary. But qualifications seem to be everything. I couldn't find a job.

After a while I got on to a Youth Training Scheme placement in an office for six months. That was great, doing something useful, chatting to the other girls, sizing up the men in the office. I really felt happy, though I knew it had to end. After six months it was back on the dole. There was another girl with me on the YTS thing – she had five O levels – but she couldn't find anything either. What chance have I?

I am bored out of my mind. Nearly 18, under my parents' feet, nothing to do. I've a boyfriend and though I don't really love him I'd marry him just to get away from home. I think I'd quite enjoy having a baby to look after – it would be something to do.

God, school had as much to do with reality as punks have to do with mods – absolutely nothing. It's all a big con, isn't it?

Fiona probably made no trouble at school, came from a 'supportive home'. Other Fionas might hope that we are asking these questions:

- What did Fiona need from school to prepare her for adult life (consider skills, attitudes, knowledge)?
- Fiona sees herself as 'useless' at school work, yet has an O level which indicates she is not. What questions should we ask about her self-esteem and how it might have been enhanced; her motivation, and how it could have been improved?
- The head of house is complimentary about Fiona. Why is Fiona now so disillusioned?
- Examination successes have not protected her father or her friend on the YTS. What conclusions might we draw?
- Her talk of marriage and babies is immature. What help does your school give in this area?

CASE THREE

Billy lies in that large group of pupils which used to be called Newsom children. He has the misfortune of having limited qualifications in an area and at a time when they have little marketable value. He has tried hard but now feels resentful, let down.

Here we go again – Monday morning, half-past nine, and a whole week to get through. I left almost exactly a year ago – not a chance of a job around here. My dad was made redundant when the pit closed about eight years ago, and hasn't worked since. It's like that for most of the men around here – either move south to the new pits in Yorkshire or settle for the dole. It'll be the same in the shipyards up the coast soon, and that'll be more people looking for the few jobs there are.

Our mam works – seems funny there's more women work than men in our village. She's really, like, the boss in our house now, so my dad's nowt.

What bugs me is the way the teachers always used to say, 'Get stuck into your work, lad, or you'll never get a job when you leave school.' Well, I'm not very bright, but I stuck in – more than some of me mates. I know four CSEs isn't much, but that was good for me. What a con. I might as well not have bothered. We're all on the dole now – them as worked and them as didn't.

What can you do around here? First two weeks after leaving, it was great. Dole money for doing nowt. Messing around on the beach, playing footer, chatting up the lasses, no school. Debbie was a canny lass – got on quite well with her really. Now she's going with Vic. Vic's dad's got a shop, so Vic's all right – he's got a job. It was all the difference with the lasses.

It's all about pride, really, isn't it? A bit of independence. A man as hasn't got a job has no pride, has he? He's nowt – even his women are better than him. I bet you can guess how my dad feels when me mam looks after the money and the spending. I get three pounds a week after paying her keep money. What can I do with that? It costs 54 pence return to get into Sunderland.

The new Leisure Centre? That's a laugh! Eighty pence to get in, plus bus fare. You can't make many trips on my three pounds. It's not meant for the likes of us – just look at the motors in the car park. We just stick in the village. The only difference between us and the old fellars sitting outside the 'Aged Miners' Cottages' is that we can run faster. We might as well be dead now.

So. Here we go again. Ten o'clock already, I might as well get up and have a bit of breakfast. Maybe I'll wander down to see Ben and Ernie. Ernie's usually cadged or nicked a few ciggies off his mam.

You'd never believe it; I'd quite fancy a morning in the craft room at school, even RE would be better than this. God, I'm fed up. Only another 50 years to go – if I'm unlucky.

- School seems to have given Billy little he appreciates. Is this inevitable?
- What might Billy have learned at school to prepare him for a situation like this?
- Do you feel happy about Billy's attitude towards his mother's essential work? About her important role in the family?
- Has Billy's self-esteem been helped at school?
- What coping skills might school have worked on to help Billy face the future with little prospect of work?
- Is Billy sufficiently aware of further education opportunities? Leisure opportunities? Self-help opportunities? Are we as teachers aware that children will need to develop these awarenesses?

CASE FOUR
Brenda represents that group of children whom we find it most difficult

to help. They often have a precocious maturity, a 'street' wisdom, that disturbs our comfortable naivety. In school terms she is a failure – no exams, no prospects. Yet she is coping with a family in the most disadvantageous circumstances. Maths and home economics? English so she can help her little sister, Anne? The motivational opportunities are high if we can find time to use them.

When my mam died I was 15, in my last year at school – a brother and two sisters younger than me and a dad who's as much use in the house as a two-year-old. It didn't really make any difference at school – I was useless and hated it anyway. When I was younger I used to like the cookery and that, but I soon began to feel that the teachers were just baby-sitting us. I don't remember ever having to decide anything for mayself – go here, come there, read this, do that. From 5 to 15 no real change. Then my mam died and I was grown up – a man and three kids to look after. Poetry and maths seemed less important than ever.

I didn't get any exams. I couldn't really have given a monkey's when that happened, though I know I'll never get a reasonable job now – Thompsons Meat Packers for me if I'm lucky.

I saw this thing on the telly; a man said people in England spend 15,000 hours in school – I can't help wondering why. All they seem to think about is exams. What about those of us who aren't good at school work? What can they do for us?

Sometimes I feel really old. I look at my brother and sister and think, 'They're going to have a better chance than me.' Anne will, she's clever, and I make sure she goes to school looking clean and lovely so the teacher will know we care. Debbie's like me, poor lass. As for Tony, well, he's a real lad. I'm not sure what he'll finish up as. Durham gaol or County Hall. I think he's got something. He's always got a smart answer, but maybe that's not a good idea in school.

My dad doesn't really care now; my mam did, but she's gone. Maybe, for her, I can make something of the other three.

– Brenda is obviously a responsible, thoughtful citizen. Could school have used that more constructively?
– How might school have prepared Brenda for her current life? What does she *need* (skills, attitudes, knowledge) that school might have offered?
– 'Go here, come there, read this, do that' to a young woman responsible for a growing family. Is our attitude to discipline well thought out? Appropriate? Flexible?
– How would we answer Brenda's questions, 'What about those of us who aren't good at school work? What can they do for us?
– Her perceptions of school values are clear – success at exams, being

clean, not being smart with answers. Do we feel comfortable with that?
- Are there other things we value that we would like her to know we value? How can we show we value such things?

CASE FIVE

Lewis represents the relatively small but inordinately influential group of children who have very low academic potential and are socially disadvantaged. They probably make up about 10 per cent of our secondary school population. One answer to such children's needs is to say that they ought to be schooled elsewhere, in special units. Jones (1975) indicates that numbers make it unlikely that that will happen, and Warnock (1978) suggests that it is not desirable anyway – we all have our ratio of Lewises. Can we help at all?

I'm 16 – left school last Easter. F-----g laugh, I hadn't been much anyway. The old fella, me dad, we don't see him. Walton gaol. He's f-----g hard. When he's home we're all scared. I'm big, but I don't cross him. There's eight in our house. Me mam – she's all right. Sticks up for us against anybody. Barbara and her little 'un – she's me sister, 18. We don't know who's the baby's dad. I reckon Babs is on the game – me dad'd kill her if he found out. There's three other lads – Davey, 14, the twins, 13, and Jeremy, 12. Me mam has lodgers – lorry drivers mostly. Some canny blokes – give you money and that – but I reckon it was one of them put Babs in the club.

School? What a f-----g waste of time. There was nowt in it for me. I used to get a bit of fun taking the piss out of the teachers. Some of them – you could see they were scared of you. We used to smash things up and fight. You could rule the playground if you had four good mates.

I was a good reader at the baby school. I can still read now if I want, but I don't. I never heard anything interesting at the big school, except talking about the match with Mr Hollins. Oh, aye, Mrs Crumbley was all right as well. She didn't look down on you; she seemed to have some respect for us.

There's no work for us, we just scrounge about. Dole money, a few drinks, nicking things. What can you do? Nobody trusts us, why should we trust them? Why should I want to get married, have some kids like me? F-----g hell! There's plenty of stuff like our Babs around, so there's no need to get married. I like punks – they don't give a f--k. The world's done nowt for us, so to hell with it.

- We have all met a Lewis. What can we offer him in school?
- What does he need to know, what feelings does he need to examine, what skills does he need to cope with his life?
- How can an ordered institution like a school cope with such an anarchic view of life?

- How do we feel about his view of women? Babs? His mother? Mrs Crumbley?
- Is *he* worth the effort involved in meeting his needs?
- Is it possible to reduce the negative effect of the maladjusted child on the other children's learning, without crushing that child?

These questions need to be answered, thought about, since they must outline all our curriculum thinking. What do our pupils need from school to cope with life in the late twentieth century? Answers must be specific to institutions and I feel no cause to apologise for listing questions rather than answers. Perhaps we have been too ready to lift educational aims from our own values and backgrounds, providing ourselves eventually with objectives that are remote from the needs of our pupils. Tackling the foregoing questions forces us to look at pupils' needs, and these should be the basis of our aims.

Approach to a response

It would perhaps be too easy to leave it at that – a list of questions, a decision by the author to say no more than 'this is the puzzle'. Very much aware of the need to arrive at school-specific answers, and therefore somewhat reluctantly, I share with the reader some of the glimmers of light I have explored with teachers in my own area. In looking at the case studies together, we gave ourselves the task of identifying pupils' needs; we forced ourselves to concentrate on needs (not society's expectations, teacher's perceptions or parental aspirations), simply children's needs. This is the list we arrived at. Children, if they are to survive and prosper as adults, need:

1. A sense of achievement.
2. A sense of independence.
3. A sense of self-esteem.
4. A sense of purpose.
5. An appreciation of 'the other half'.
6. Values.
7. Skill in personal relationships.
8. Skill in making decisions.
9. Activity/involvement.
10. Knowledge of helping agencies outside of school.
11. Personal attention.
12. Information/vocational guidance.
13. An opportunity to discover their own needs.

14. A sense of capacity for joy.
15. To see self as worth-while, not the tool of others.
16. Less academic pressure.
17. To see learning as worth while in itself.
18. Awareness of leisure opportunities.
19. Contact with their own feelings; sensitivity.
20. Cushions removed.
21. To see that unemployment is not a personal failure.
22. To be instrumental, not a victim.
23. To have money management skill.

There has been no attempt to categorise here, no imposing priorities. The list is compiled by a group of teacher colleagues after reading the five cases in this chapter. Our own work continued into an attempt to refine our 'needs' list into curriculum aims. A careful analysis of the curriculum strongly indicates a tendency to favour the academic development of the Clives, at the expense of all else. That situation must be positively embraced if we want it. If, on the other hand, we regard other children as worth-while, then our investment of resources, rewards, personnel and time must be as committed. The issues identified above as central to children's education are conspicuous by their absence from the National Curriculum, which speaks volumes about the underlying philosophy of that curriculum. We will learn much about our educational philosophy by considering the following issues.

What ought we to teach? What helps our pupils?

Identify how developmental and remedial responses could be made for each child in the cases outlined, with reference to the following areas:

– What *skills* do Clive, Fiona, Billy, Brenda and Lewis need
  Academically.
  Socially.
  Emotionally.
  How can school help? What help does school need?

– What *attitudes* do Clive, Fiona, Billy, Brenda and Lewis need to
  analyse with reference towards
  School and work.
  Self.
  Others.

- What *knowledge* do Clive, Fiona, Billy, Brenda and Lewis need about
  Themselves.
  The world in which they live.
  The world of tomorrow.
  The world of yesterday.
  Opportunities for themselves.

A school staff will disagree profoundly in seeking to analyse these issues, but at least they are the *issues*. A planned system of pastoral care cannot emerge unless we face these issues squarely. From a management point of view, we are trying to change from a curriculum designed to meet the needs of an industrial society to a curriculum designed to meet the needs of a post-industrial society; it will involve looking very carefully at the skills our pupils will need, not merely to survive but to prosper in that society. Having identified pupils' needs (and being open to continual reappraisal and revision), a planning group can move to the distillation of aims from those needs; broad whole school aims to be refined eventually into precise objectives, lesson by lesson. In formulating the aims, we can then analyse carefully the extent to which (a) school ethos and (b) the individual classroom pedagogical styles facilitate or impede them. The more radical approach of 'whole school' analysis can be tackled less traumatically by individual teachers tackling change more gradually, classroom by classroom. What are the blocks? Time? Inadequate resources? Split site? Severely disruptive children? This will take us back to the management team who are challenged just as ferociously as the classroom teachers by the new situation. No one in education can opt out.

Bibliography

Abercrombie, M L (1979) *Aims and Techniques of Group Teaching* Society for Research into Higher Education

Argyle, M (1983) *The Psychology of Interpersonal Behaviour*, 4th edn, Penguin, Harmondsworth

Argyle, M (1988) *Bodily Communication* Methuen

Balogh, J (1982) *Profile Reports for School Leavers* Longman, Harlow

Beard, R M (1969) *An Outline of Piaget's Developmental Psychology for Teachers* Routledge and Kegan Paul, London

Bell, A (1805) *An Experiment in Education*, 2nd edn, Cadell and Davies, London; quoted in Smith, F (1931) *A History of English Elementary Education 1760–1902* University of London Press, p 79

Best, R E, Jarvis, C and Ribbins, P (1977) Pastoral care: concept and process, *British Journal of Educational Studies* pp 124–5, June

Black, P J (The Black Report). See DES *National Curriculum*

Blocher, D H *et al.* (1971) *Guidance Systems: An Introduction to Student Personnel Work* Ronald Press, New York

Blocher, D H (1974) *Developmental Counselling* Ronald Press, New York

Blomberg, A and Golembiewski, R T (1976) *Learning and Change in Groups* Penguin, Harmondsworth

Borba, M C and Borba, C (1978) *Self Esteem: A Classroom Affair* Harper and Row, San Francisco

Bradshaw, F F (1936) The scope and aim of a personnel program, *Educational Research* XVII

Brammer, L M and Shostrum, E L (1968) *Therapeutic Psychology*, 2nd edn, Prentice-Hall, Englewood Cliffs, NJ

Brammer, L M and Shostrum, E L (1976) *Therapeutic Psychology*, 3rd edn, Prentice-Hall, Englewood Cliffs, NJ

Brammer, L M and Shostrum, E L (1982) *Therapeutic Psychology*, 4th edn, Prentice-Hall, Englewood Cliffs, NJ

Brandes, D and Ginnis, P (1986) *A Guide to Student-centred Learning* Blackwell

Brandes, D and Phillips, H (1979) *The Gamesters Handbook* Hutchinson, London

Briggs, D C (1970) *Your Child's Self Esteem* Doubleday, New York

Burns, R B (1979) *The Self-Concept: Theory, Measurement, Development and Behaviour* Longman, Harlow

Burns, R B (1982) *Self Concept Development and Education* Holt, Rinehart and Winston, London

Carkhuff, R R and Berenson, B G (1977) *Beyond Counselling and Therapy*, 2nd edn, Holt, Rinehart and Winston, New York

Carlson, E (1969) *Learning Through Games* Public Affairs Press, Washington DC

Cartwright, C A and Cartwright, G P (1974) *Developing Observation Skills* McGraw-Hill, New York

Cicourel, A V and Kitsuse, J (1963) *The Educational Decision-makers* Bobbs-Merril, Indianapolis

Clegg, A and Megson, B (1973) *Children in Distress*, 2nd edn, Penguin, Harmondsworth

Cleugh, M F (1971) *Discipline and Morale in School and College: A Study of Group Feeling* Tavistock, London

Coffield, F J, Borrill, C and Marshall, S (1986) *Growing Up at the Margins* OUP, Milton Keynes

Coleman, J C (1980) *The Nature of Adolescence* McOwen

Coleman, J S (1961) *The Adolescent Society* Free Press, New York

Coopersmith, S (1967) *Antecedents of Self Esteem* Freeman, San Francisco

CRAC (1971–4) *Your Choice* Cambridge Careers Research Advisory Centre

Craft, M, Raynor, J and Cohen, L (1980) *Linking Home and School*, 3rd end, Longman, Harlow

Davie, R, Butler, N and Goldstein, H (1972) *From Birth to Seven* Longman, London

Daws, P D (1976) *Early Days – A Personal Review of the Beginning of Counselling in English Education during the Decade 1964–1974* Careers Research Advisory Council

Dent, H C (1949) *Secondary Education for All*, Routledge and Kegan Paul, London (quoted in Silver, H (ed) 1973) *Equal Opportunity in Education* Methuen, London)

DES (1973) *Careers Education in Secondary Schools, Survey 18* HMSO

DES (1977a) *Assessment – Why, What and How?* HMSO

DES (1977b) *Curriculum 11–16* HMSO

DES (1977c) *Education in Schools: A Consultative Document* Cmnd 6869, HMSO

DES (1979) *Aspects of Secondary Education in England* HMSO

DES (1980) *A View of the Curriculum* HMSO

DES (1981) *The School Curriculum* HMSO

DES (1984) *Records of Achievement: A Statement of Policy* HMSO

DES (1985) *Better Schools* HMSO

DES (1985) *Records of Achievement at 16. Some Samples of Current Practice* HMSO

DES (1987a) *Curriculum Matters: Personal and Social Education from 5–16* HMSO

DES (1987b) *Good Behaviour and Discipline in Schools* HMSO

DES (1987c) *Records of Achievement: An Interim Report* HMSO

DES (1987d) *Teaching as a Career* HMSO

DES (1988) *National Curriculum: Task Group on Assessment and Testing* (The Black Report) HMSO

DES (1988a) *National Curriculum: Task Group on Assessment and Testing. Three Supplementary Reports* HMSO

DES (1988b) *Working Together for the Protection of Children from Abuse* Circular No 4/88

DHSS (1974) *Report of the Committee of Inquiry into the Care and Supervision Provided in Relation to Maria Colwell* HMSO

DHSS (1988) *Working Together for the Protection of Children from Abuse* Circular No 26/88

Dunham, J (1984) *Stress in Teaching* Croom Helm, London

East Sussex County Council (1975) *Children at Risk* East Sussex County Council

Egan, G (1975) *The Skilled Helper – A Model for Systematic Helping and Interpersonal Relating* Brookes Cole, Monterey, California (Text accompanied by a separate skill development manual.)

Egan, G (1986) *The Skilled Helper: A Systematic Approach to Effective Helping* Brookes-Cole Publishing, Monterey

Egan, G and Cowan, M A (1979) *People in Systems: A Model for Development in the Human Service Professions and Education* Wadsworth, Belmont

Elton Committee (in session, 1988) *Enquiry into Discipline in Schools*

Eraut, M (1981) Accountability and evaluation (in Simon, B, Taylor, W (eds) *Education in the Eighties: the Central Issues* Batsford Academic and Educational)

Erikson, E H (1965) *Childhood and Society* Penguin, Harmondsworth

Erikson, E H (1968) *Identity: Youth and Crisis* Faber and Faber, London

Everard, K B (1984) *Management in Comprehensive Schools: What Can Be Learned from Industry?* Centre for the Study of Comprehensive Schools, University of York

Everard, K B (1986) *Developing Management in Schools* Blackwell, Oxford

Eysenck, H J (1953) *Uses and Abuses of Psychology* Penguin, London

Eysenck, H J (1965) The effects of psychotherapy. *International Journal of Psychiatry* 1, 97–178

Fletcher, A (1980) *Guidance in Schools* Aberdeen University Press

Freud, A (1968) *The Ego and Mechanisms of Defence* Hogarth Press, London

Garforth, D and MacKintosh, L H (1986) *Profiling: A User's Manual* Stanley Thomas, Cheltenham

Gelatt, H B (1962) Decision-making: a conceptual frame of reference for counselling, *Journal of Counselling Psychology* 9, 3, pp 240–5

Graham, D (1972) *Moral Learning and Development* Batsford, London

Gruff, W N and Lazerson, M (1981) 'Vocational solutions to youth problems: the persistent frustrations of the American experience, *Educational Analysis* Vol 3, No 2, Falmer Press

Hamblin, D H (1974) *The Teacher and Counselling* Blackwell, Oxford

Hamblin, D H (1976) The counsellor and strategies for the treatment of disturbed children in the secondary school, *British Journal of Guidance and Counselling* pp 172–89, January

Hamblin, D H (1978) *The Teacher and Pastoral Care* Blackwell, Oxford

Hansard (on school records) (1978) 954, 229–38

Hargreaves, D H (1967) *Social Relations in the Secondary School* Routledge and Kegan Paul, London

Hargreaves, D H (1976a) *Deviance in the Classroom*, Routledge and Kegan Paul, London

Hargreaves, D H (1976b) The Real Battle for the Classroom, *New Society*, 29 January

Hargreaves, D H (1976c) Learning to be deviant in school, in Roberts, T *The Circumstances of Learning* University of Manchester Studies in Education

Hargreaves, D H (1982) *The Challenge for the Comprehensive Schools: Culture, Curriculum and Community* Routledge, Kegan Paul, London

Hargreaves, D H (1984) *Improving Secondary Schools: Report of the Hargreaves Committee*, ILEA

Havighurst, R J (1953) *Human Development Education* Longman, Harlow

Haviland, J (ed) (1988) *Take Care, Mr Baker* Fourth Estate

Hawton, K and Catalan, J (1987) *Attempted Suicide* Oxford University Press

Heath, D H (1977) *Maturity and Competence* Gardner, New York

Hemmings, J (1980) *The Betrayal of Youth: Secondary Education Must Change* Marion Boyars, London

Hopson, B and Hough, P (1976) The need for personal and social education in secondary schools and further education, *British Journal of Guidance and Counselling*, January

Hopson, B and Scally, M (1979) *NICEC Training Bulletin*, Hatfield Polytechnic, Bayfordbury House, Hertford

Hopson, B and Scally, M (1981) *Lifeskills Teaching* McGraw-Hill, London

Hopson, B and Scally, M (1986) *Lifeskills Teaching Programme* Lifeskills Associates, Leeds

Insel, P M and Jacobson, L F (1977) *What Do You Expect? An Enquiry into Self-Fulfilling Prophecies* Cummings, Menlo Park

International Labour Organisation (1981) quoted in the *Guardian*, 4 July

Jackson, S (1971) *A Teacher's Guide to Tests and Testing* Longman, Harlow

James Report (1972) Committee of Inquiry into Teacher Education and Training, HMSO

Johnson, D and Ransome, E (1983) *Family and Schools* Croom Helm, London

Jones, N J (1975) Emotionally Disturbed Children in Ordinary Schools, *British Journal of Guidance and Counselling* pp 146–57, July

Jones, N J (1983) An integrated approach to special educational needs, *Forum 25*, 2, 36–9

Jones-Davies, C (1976) *The Disruptive Pupil in the Secondary School* Ward Lock Educational, London

Kanfer, F H and Goldstein, A P (1975) *Helping People Change* Pergamon, Oxford

Keat, D B (1979) *Multi-Modal Therapy with Children* Pergamon, Oxford

Kellmer-Pringle, M (1965) *Deprivation and Education* Longman, Harlow

Kirk, R F (1987) *Learning in Action: Activities for Personal and Group Development* Blackwell, Oxford

Kohlberg, L (1977) Moral development, ego development and psycho-educational practices in Miller, P (ed) *Developmental Theory* Department of Education, Minnesota

Krumboltz, J D and Thoresen, C E (1976) *Counselling Methods* Holt,

Rinehart and Winston, New York

Lacey, C (1970) *Hightown Grammar: The School as a Social System* Manchester University Press

Lang, P (1988) (ed) *Thinking about PSE in the Primary School* Blackwell, Oxford

Law, W (1979) *Structures, Dynamics and Issues for Guidance and the School Curriculum* Proceedings of IRTAC Conference, Cambridge

Law, W (1984) *Uses and Abuses of Profiling* Harper and Row, London

Law, W and Watts, A G (1977) *Schools, Careers and Community* CIO Publishing, London

Lawrence, D (1973) *Improved Reading Through Counselling* Ward Lock, London

Lowenstein, L (1975) *Violent and Disruptive Behaviour in Schools* National Association of Schoolmasters, Hemel Hempstead

McBeath, J, Mearns, D and Smith, M (1986) *Home from School* Jordanhill College of Education

McClure, J S (1981) *Education Documents: The School Curriculum* DES HMSO

McGuiness, J B (1977) MA dissertation, University of Durham (unpublished)

McGuiness, J B (1982) *Planned Pastoral Care* McGraw-Hill, London

McGuiness, J B (1983) Secondary education for all? in Colfield, F J and Goodings, R D (eds) *Sacred Cows in Education* Edinburgh University Press

McGuiness, J and Craggs, D (1986) Disruption as a school-generated problem in Tattum, D (ed) *Management of Disruptive Pupil Behaviour in Schools* John Wiley and Sons

McGuiness, J and Gilliland, J (1989) Counselling and special educational needs in Jones, N J (ed) *The Special Educational Needs Yearbook* Falmer Press

Macmillan, A and Kolvin, I (1977) Behaviour modification in educational settings, *Journal of the Association of Workers with Maladjusted Children*, 5, 1

McMullen, T (1978) *Innovative Practices in Secondary Education* OECD, Luxembourg

Mahler, C (1969) *Group Counselling in the Schools* Houghton Mifflin, Boston

Manpower Services Commission (1986) *TVEI Review* MSC, London

Mead, M (1974) *Coming of Age in Samoa* Penguin, Harmondsworth

Merritt, G (1982) *World Out of Work* Collins

Milner, P (1974) *Counselling in Education* Dent, London

Minuchin, S (1974) *Families and Family Therapy* Tavistock, London

(also as Soc. Sc. Pbs. 1977)

Moore, B M (1970) *Guidance in Comprehensive Schools* NFER, Windsor

Morris, B (1972) *Objectives and Perspectives in Education* Routledge and Kegan Paul, London

Musgrave, F (1964) *Youth and Social Order* Routledge and Kegan Paul, London

Musgrave, F (1967) *Childhood and Adolescence* Schools Council Working Paper 12, pp 48–59, HMSO

NAS-UWT (1974) *Discipline in Schools* National Association of Schoolmasters, Hemel Hempstead

NAS-UWT (1975) *Stress in Schools* National Association of Schoolmasters, Hemel Hempstead

Nash, P (1968) *Authority and Freedom in Education* Wiley, New York

National Association of EWOS (1974) Working Paper on Truancy

Newsom Report (1963) *Half Our Future* HMSO

NFER (1980) *Lewis Counselling Inventory* NFER, Windsor

NFER (1986) *Catalogue of Tests for Educational Guidance and Assessment* NFER, Windsor (annually)

Nicholson, E (1970) Success and admission criteria for potentially successful risks, *Project Report*, Brown University, Providence RI and Ford Foundation, New York

Patterson, C H (1974) Humanistic education, *British Journal of Guidance and Counselling* pp 2–13, January

Perls, F S and Stevens, J O (1971) *Gestalt Therapy Verbatim* Bantam, New York

Perls, F S (1973) *Gestalt Approach and Eye Witness to Therapy* Bantam, New York

Piaget, J and Inhelder, B (1958) *The Growth of Logical Awareness from Childhood to Adolescence* Routledge and Kegan Paul, London

Pidgeon, D and Yates, A (1968) *An Introduction to Educational Measurement* Routledge and Kegan Paul, London

Piven, F F and Cloward, R A (1972) *Regulating the Poor* Tavistock, London

Plowden Report (1967) *Children and Their Primary Schools* HMSO

Rath, L E and Simon, S B (1978) *Values and Teaching* Merrill Publishing Company, Ohio

Reich, B and Adcock, C (1976) *Values, Attitudes and Behaviour Change* Methuen, London

Richardson, J (1979) Objections to personal counselling in schools, *British Journal of Guidance and Counselling* pp 129–43, January

Rogers, C R (1942) *Counselling and Psychotherapy* Houghton Mifflin, Boston

Rogers, C R (1962) *On Becoming a Person: A Therapist's View of Psychotherapy* Constable, London

Rogers, C R (1965) *Client-Centred Therapy* Constable, London

Rogers, C R (1969) *Freedom to Learn: A View of What Education Might Become* C E Merrill Publishing Co, Columbus, Ohio

Rogers, C R (1971) *Encounter Groups* Allen Lane, London

Rogers, C R (1983) *Freedom to Learn for the Eighties* Merrill Publishing Company, Ohio

Rosenberg, M (1965) *Society and the Adolescent Self Image* Princeton University Press, Princeton

Rosenthal, R and Jacobson, L (1966) Teacher expectancies: determinants of pupil IQ gains, *Psychological Reports* 19, pp 115–18 (Bobbs-Merrill)

Rowntree, D (1978) *Assessing Students: How Shall We Know Them?* Kogan Page, London

Rutter, M, Maughan, B, Mortimore, P and Ouston, J (1979) *Fifteen Thousand Hours* Open Books, Shepton Mallet

Samuels, Shirley C (1977) *Enhancing the Self Concept in Early Childhood* New York Human Sciences Press

Savage, R D (1968) *Psychometric Assessment of the Individual Child* Penguin, Harmondsworth

Schools Council (1979) *Record of Personal Achievement* (compiled by Swales) Pamphlet 16

Schostak, J F (1983) *Maladjusted Schooling: Deviance, Social Control and Individuality in Secondary Schooling* Falmer Press, London

Secondary Heads Association (1979) Letter from the President, *Guardian*, 11 September

Shaw, M C (1973) *School Guidance Systems* Houghton Mifflin, Boston

Sherif, M and Sherif, C (1964) *Reference Groups: Exploration into Conformity and Deviation of Adolescents* Harper and Row, New York

Shertzer, B and Stone, S C (1971) *Fundamentals of Guidance* Houghton Mifflin, Boston

Silberman, C (1970) *Crisis in the Classroom* Random House, New York

Simon B (1988) *Bending the Rules: The Baker 'Reform' of Education* Lawrence and Wishart, London

Simon, S B *et al.* (1972) *Values Clarification* Hart, New York

Simon, S B and Clark, J (1975) *Values Clarification* Pennant Press, La Mesa, California

Snygg, A W and Combs, D (1959) *Individual Behaviour* Harper and Row, New York

Sockett, H T (1976) *Designing the Curriculum* Open Books, Shepton Mallet

Spence, S (1980) *Social Skills Training with Children and Adolescents* NFER, Windsor

Sprinthall, N A (1981) A new model for research in the service of guidance and counselling, *Personnel and Guidance Journal* 59, 8, April

Summerfield Report (1968) *Psychologists in Education Services* HMSO

Super, D E (1957) *The Psychology of Careers* Harper and Row, London

Tansey, P (ed) (1971) *Educational Aspects of Simulation* McGraw-Hill, London

Taylor, J and Walford, R (1974) *Simulation in the Classroom* Penguin, Harmondsworth

Taylor, M T (1976) Teacher perceptions of pupils, *Research in Education* pp 25–35, November

Taylor, W (1978) *Research and Reform in Teacher Education* NFER, Windsor

Tibble, T W (1964) *Adults and Adolescents, Group Discussions on Relationships and Problems of Communication* UNESCO/NEF

Thomas, J B (1973) *Self Concept in Psychology and Education: A Review of Research* NFER

Toffler, A (1971) *Future Shock* Pan, London

Truax, C B and Carkhuff, R R (1967) *Towards Effective Counselling and Psychotherapy* Aldine Publishing, Chicago

Walford, R S (1969) *Games in Geography* Longman, Harlow

Walker, W (1932) *The School as an Organisation* Wiley, New York

Wall, W D (1977) *Constructive Education for Adolescents* Harrap, London

Waller, W (1932) *The Sociology of Teaching* Wiley, New York

Warnock Report (1978) *Meeting Special Educational Needs* HMSO

Warren, N G and Johoda, M (1973) *Attitudes: Selected Readings*, 2nd edn, Penguin, Harmondsworth

Waskow, I E (1963) Counsellor attitudes and client behaviour, *Journal of Counselling Psychology* 27, pp 405–12

Watts, A G (1978) Implications of school-leaver unemployment for careers education in schools, *Journal of Curriculum Studies* 10, 2, June

White, R and Lippitt, R (1968) Leader behaviour and member reaction in three social climates in Cartwright, D and Zanders, A (eds) *Group Dynamics: Research or Theory* pp 318–35, Tavistock, London

Index